NEA
EARLY CHILDHOOD
EDUCATION SERIES

Developmentally Appropriate Teaching in Early Childhood

Curriculum, Implementation, Evaluation

Dominic F. Gullo

A NATIONAL EDUCATION ASSOCIATION
P U B L I C A T I O N

Printing History
    First Printing: May 1992

Note

The opinions expressed in this publication should not be construed as representing the policy or position of the National Education Association. Materials published by the NEA Professional Library are intended to be discussion documents for teachers who are concerned with specialized interests of the profession.

Library of Congress Cataloging-in-Publication Data

Gullo, Dominic F.
    Developmentally appropriate teaching in early childhood :
curriculum, implementation, evaluation / by Dominic F. Gullo.
        p.   cm. — (NEA Early childhood education series)
    Includes bibliographical references.
    ISBN 0-8106-0362-4
    1. Early childhood education—United States.   2. Early childhood
education—United States—Curricula.   3. Early childhood education-
-United States—Parent participation.   4. Early childhood education-
-United States—Evaluation.   5. Child development—United States.
I. Title.   II. Series: Early childhood education series (Washington,
D.C.)
    LB1139.25.G85   1991
    372.21'0973—dc20   91-24447
                                                                        CIP

This book is dedicated to the young children of this world—that they may all develop to their optimal potential. And to all the adults in their lives who strive to make this happen. Specifically, I dedicate this book to Matthew and Timothy, who not only taught me almost everything I know about children, but also made me aware of those things I don't know—and to Jeanne, who learned with me.

CONTENTS

Acknowledgments 7

Chapter 1. Introduction 9

Chapter 2. Match Early Childhood Education
Practices to How Children Learn. 13
Processing Information 14
Constructing Knowledge 19
Cognitive Characteristics in Early
Childhood 26
Implications for the Curriculum 30

Chapter 3. Create a Classroom Environment That
Facilitates Learning and Development 35
Objects in the Environment 35
Interaction in the Environment. 38
Learning Contexts in the Environment. 41
Individualizing Through the Environment . . . 44
Characteristics of the Learning Environment . . 47

Chapter 4. Continuity of Child Development and the
Implications for Teaching Practice 51
The Gift of Time. 54

Chapter 5. The Role of Parent Involvement in the
Early Childhood Curriculum. 57
Types of Parent Involvement 58
Benefits of Parent Involvement. 61
Obstacles to Parent Involvement 61
Promoting Parent Involvement in Schools . . . 63

Chapter 6. Ongoing Evaluation as a Factor in Decision
Making and Curriculum Development . . . 65
Testing and School Readiness. 65

Effects of Schooling Decisions Based on
    Gift of Time 66
Teaching, Curriculum, and the Gift of Time . . 68
The Right Problem but the Wrong Solution . . 69
Evaluation from a Developmental Perspective . 71
Alternative Assessment 75

Chapter 7. Conclusion 77
The Early Childhood Curriculum:
    A Transactional Process 77

Appendix 79

References 89

ACKNOWLEDGMENTS

I would like to acknowledge all of my students who listened patiently, and sometimes intently, over the years as my ideas became focused and finally jelled (in my mind, at least).

I would particularly like to thank Kris Stromberg, whose ideas you'll find in the integrated unit at the end of this publication.

Finally, I would like to thank a dear friend and my mentor, Nicholas Anastasiow, who not only taught me how to ask questions, but also how to seek the truth and enjoy life along the way.

The Author

Dominic F. Gullo is Professor of Early Childhood Education at the University of Wisconsin, Milwaukee.

The Advisory Panel

Craig H. Hart, Assistant Professor of Child Development and Early Childhood Education, School of Human Ecology, Louisiana State University, Baton Rouge

Rebecca S. Landers, Special Education Teacher, Haleyville Elementary School, Alabama

Karen S. Lewis, Kindergarten Teacher, Lincoln School, West Chicago

Sandra L. Moran, Kindergarten Curriculum Developer with the California Mentor Program, Twentynine Palms Elementary School

Chapter 1

INTRODUCTION

Early childhood education is an exciting and dynamic profession. In recent years the profession has undergone a number of significant transitions through which it has gained attention and national interest. Several factors have contributed to this rekindled focus. These include increased knowledge about child development, particularly how children learn; increases in the number of children attending early childhood education programs at earlier ages; and changing family structures, functions, and needs, as well as a changing society, in general. Each of these factors has contributed uniquely, as well as collectively, to contemporary early childhood education philosophy and practice.

Early childhood education generally refers to programs appropriate for children ages birth to eight-years-old. These programs may be housed in various locations, ranging from private facilities (e.g., child care centers, nursery schools, hospitals, etc.) to agencies (e.g., Head Start), to public school programs. In order to establish a common frame of reference regarding early childhood, it may be appropriate to define its use in this book. Early childhood may be defined from three different but related perspectives: (1) from a chronological age perspective, (2) from a developmental perspective, or (3) as in the traditional school setting, by grade level.

As mentioned briefly above, early childhood is defined chronologically as those ages between birth and eight-years-old. These are the years of greatest dependency on others and according to some (Scarr 1976), it is the period of greatest biological similarity with respect to the course of development, particularly cognitive development. In addition to recognizing that this age span consists of many universal developmental traits, it also has been recognized as being uniquely different from those ages beyond the eighth year. There is, in fact, a biophysical change in the brain that occurs at around age seven or eight (Anastasiow 1986). The maturation and resulting integration of particular brain functions at this age, make it possible for children to learn things at age seven or eight that were not possible at age five.

The developmental definition of early childhood is understandably very closely related to the chronological definition. According to Piaget (1963), a developmental child psychologist whose work has significantly influenced and shaped the field of early childhood education, the parameters of early childhood are captured by the sensorimotor and preoperational periods of cognitive development. These two stages of cognitive development include approximately the first eight years of life. These periods are characterized by the unique manner in which children process information, construct knowledge, and solve problems. As a result, children in this developmental period require specialized instruction and learning environments.

Differences between the chronological and developmental definitions of early childhood are characterized best by children whose developmental timetables are either accelerated or delayed. Children who are chronologically beyond the early childhood years, but whose cognitive development is within the preoperational stage, are best served by teaching techniques and materials appropriate for early childhood education. Conversely, some early childhood education strategies may not be appropriate for children beyond preoperations, but whose age falls within the defined early childhood years.

Finally, early childhood education can be defined by grade level (NASBE 1988). This is particularly appropriate in the school setting. Early childhood education covers those grade levels between prekindergarten and third grade. Increasingly, more and more schools are including prekindergarten as part of their regular academic programs. These programs generally start at age four; however, some may begin as early as age three in the regular classroom.

In this book, early childhood education is explored using the knowledge base from which developmentally appropriate early childhood practice has been shown to facilitate development and learning in young children. Each chapter focuses on a principle of sound practice that is grounded in research. In Chapter 2, the guiding principle is to *match early childhood education practices to the ways children learn.* Factors affecting children's development and the unique characteristics of children's thinking in the early childhood years are explored. Chapter 3 addresses the implementation of developmentally appropriate curriculum practices through structuring and organizing the learning environment. The guiding principle here is to *create a classroom environment that encourages exploration and facilitates learning and development.* Characteristics of the environment and materials from which children process information, construct knowledge, and problem solve will be the focus of the chapter. The guiding principle in Chapter 4 is to *view the age range from five- to eight-years-old as a continuum of development rather than as discrete grade levels,* and curricular and instructional strategies for dealing with the similarities and differences found across this age span are discussed. The guiding principle of Chapter 5 is to *consider parent involvement as a critical and essential element in the early childhood curriculum.* The chapter focuses on the role of parent involvement in early childhood and describes the benefits of parent involvement for children, parents, teachers, and schools in general. Chapter 6 delves into the relationship between evaluation, the curriculum, and the child. The guiding principle for this chapter is to *use ongoing evaluation for decision making and curriculum development.* Finally, a transactional approach to teaching in early childhood in order to achieve optimal learning and development, and the implications of such an approach are discussed in Chapter 7.

Each chapter has a similar format. Along with the pertinent research, concrete examples and implications for practice are discussed. Much of the information provided in this book is new. It is hoped that the information that is *not* new is presented in such a manner as to provide new insights and reaffirmation for current practices.

Chapter 2

MATCH EARLY CHILDHOOD EDUCATION PRACTICES TO HOW CHILDREN LEARN

One evening while coloring, a five-year-old boy asked his father to show him how to make a capital *L*. The father proceeded to make the *L* for his son on a separate piece of paper. Upon looking at the *L* that his father had made, the five-year-old admonished the father that he didn't think his *L* was in correct form. The boy remarked that the *L* sort of looked right but that the dots were missing. At that point the father tried to convince his son that *L's* did not have dots, and that only small *i's* and *j's* had dots. Unconvinced, the boy took the paper upon which the father had so carefully modeled the capital *L* and proceeded to demonstrate to his father just where the dots belonged. He put a dot at the top of the *L*, another at the right angle where the lines forming the letter meet, and another at the end of the horizontal smaller line. "There," the boy said with satisfaction, "*that's* how we learned to make them in school!"

This story illustrates just how children who are in the preoperational stage of development process information, construct knowledge, and problem solve about objects and events in their environment. In many instances, teachers of young children may not know exactly what their children are focusing on in the learning environment. Many times children at this developmental level will interpret information in a different way than intended or in a different manner than adults or older children do. Because children in the preoperational stage of cognitive development process information, construct knowledge, and problem solve in a qualitatively different manner, it is imperative that early childhood educators *match early childhood education practices to the ways children learn.*

13

PROCESSING INFORMATION

Children's success in detecting and understanding the information that is contained in an environmental event will depend on how efficiently and completely the information is processed. Information is processed through attention, perception, memory, thinking, and problem solving (Yussen and Santrock 1982). How efficiently or completely the information is processed, or it if is processed at all, will determine the nature of the response to the event. In some cases, this may include no response at all. Children in early childhood settings are in the preoperational stage of cognitive development. As a result, they will process information differently than those children in other stages of development, and therefore we might expect that they will respond to environmental stimuli in a different manner. Following is a discussion of how being in preoperation affects children's ability to process information.

Attention

Attention may be defined as the process of noticing an event or "tuning in" to sensory information. Before children *can* respond to an environmental event, they must first recognize that the event exists. Jackson, Robinson, and Dale (1976) describe five factors that determine the focus and duration of a young child's attention.

First, young children attend to information that they can discriminate. This implies that young children cannot attend to information that they cannot see or hear. It is important, therefore, that the adults who are participating in the child's world remain aware of the fact that often the child cannot, from their point of view, see and/or hear things in the same manner that the adult or older children do. This is because the child is *egocentric*, a concept that will be discussed later. As a result, the child may respond in a manner that the adult does not expect, or may not respond at all to what the adult *presumes* the child is paying attention to.

14

Second, children seem to be more attentive at some times than at others. At the same time, some children are simply more attentive than other children, all the time. Factors that seem to affect attention are fatigue, overexcitedness, or distress. A child who is in one of these states might have difficulty attending.

Third, the physical qualities and background of an event may influence whether a child will attend to that event. Size, shape, complexity, and loudness are all event characteristics that affect attention. The more intense each of these characteristics is for any event, the greater the likelihood that it will be attended to.

Fourth, there is greater likelihood that an event will be attended to if it has meaning for the child. Children learn that not only do entire events have meaning but that within an event there are aspects of the event that may be ignored (Pick 1965; Pick, Christy, and Frankel 1972).

Fifth, attention will be determined by the way it fits into the child's existing knowledge of the world's events. Children tend to pay attention to events that are slightly unfamiliar or novel (Kagan 1972; Piaget 1963), yet if too unfamiliar, the event may be ignored because it is not recognizable as an event.

Changes in the ability to pay attention continue beyond the very early years and extend into the sixth and seventh year of life (Yussen and Santrock 1983). These changes in the ability to attend have an effect on children's ability to extract information from their environment (Hagen and Hale 1973; Pick, Frankel, and Hess 1976).

Perception

Once children have attended to an environmental event, they must make some sense out of it. Perception may be defined as the cognitive process whereby one recognizes and interprets meaning from that which was picked up by the sensory receptors (Mussen et al. 1984; Yussen and Santrock 1982).

According to Mussen et al. (1984), the major goal of the perception process is to understand environmental events, and to match what is perceived to some cognitive unit already present in the child. These environmental events include: (a) physical objects that are characteristically static (e.g., house, table, rock); (b) events that are characteristically dynamic and occur over time (e.g., a dog chasing a bone as opposed to a dog bringing a newspaper); (c) two-dimensional representations of three-dimensional events; (d) symbolic representations of events (e.g., words, numbers, language); and (e) body sensations (e.g., increased heartbeat and muscle tension).

There are many developmental changes that take place in perception throughout childhood. As children mature, they acquire more knowledge about the world, leading to more efficient use of perception. As they become more knowledgeable about information contained in environmental events, less information or less redundancy is required to perceive them. In a classic study, Gollin (1962) investigated how much information was required by individuals at different ages in order for them to identify objects from line drawings. He found that the amount of information required to recognize an object was directly related to age. The younger the child, the more information he or she required to identify the object in the drawing.

As children grow older, they also change in how they perceive physical characteristics of objects. Objects in the environment have many physical properties, e.g., size, shape, color. Which one of these attributes of the object is the most significant feature for the child? It has been conjectured that different children have different predispositions toward which attributes of objects they will focus on (Gullo 1985; Yussen and Santrock 1982). There seems to be individual differences in preference of these features for individual children. These differences may be attributed to differences in biological development (maturation) or to differences in the physical and/or social experiences to which they have been exposed.

Similarly, it has been shown that younger children have a more holistic perception of objects (Kemler 1982; Kember and Smith 1979). Younger children, when asked to classify objects, tend to group objects according to some overall idea of sameness rather than to look at the underlying attributes. The reverse is true for older children. For example, younger children might group objects that are the same color but are different shapes and sizes. Older children will group according to all of the attributes, thus are capable of categorizing on multiple levels. The younger child seems incapable of making these finer perceptual discriminations, and is unable to discriminate on more than one feature at a time. The reasons for this will be discussed later, when the cognitive characteristics of preoperational children are described.

Finally, perception changes with experience. The more experiences one has, the more meaningful the perception of that event will have for the child. Much evidence for this has been found in transcultural research. In our culture, children have many experiences interpreting two-dimensional events. Children who either lack this type of experience (Hochberg and Brook 1962) or who are from cultures where this type of experience was not normally available to them (Hudson 1960, 1967; Mundy-Castle 1966) had difficulty in recognizing the meaning of common objects or events represented in two dimensions. These findings have significance for the children in our early childhood classrooms, which will be discussed later in this chapter.

Memory

Memory is defined as the retention of information over time (Yussen and Santrock 1982). There are two types of memory: (1) short-term memory (STM), and (2) long-term memory (LTM). In short-term memory, information is processed and stored only temporarily, usually for immediate use. This type of memory is useful in aiding one to perform everyday activities. In the early childhood classroom, children need STM to remember instructions for classroom activities, following directions, and answering questions after hearing a story. STM may last from a few seconds to a minute. Studies have shown that STM across a wide spectrum of ages in childhood remains fairly similar (Cole, Frankel, and Sharpe 1971; Kail 1979).

The second type of memory, long-term memory, is a process whereby information may be stored and retrieved for up to a lifetime. It is in LTM that one stores information and experiences about the world that will be drawn upon for daily use, or from time to time, over a long period. Yussen and Santrock (1982) note that there are developmental differences in children's ability to store information in LTM or to shift information from STM to LTM, with older children being more adept in this process.

Jackson et al. (1976), outlined four conditions that may determine whether a young child is likely to remember information. Children are more likely to remember information—

1. If it is familiar, meaningful, and contains an internal organization of its own (e.g., a group of items with similar characteristics);
2. When they have been actively involved with the material that is to be remembered;
3. If they have had repeated exposure to the material that is to be remembered; and
4. If the information is of interest to them and draws their attention.

Thinking

Mussen et al. (1984) describe thinking as the process whereby a child reflects on the information being processed in order to assess and evaluate it before responding. Some children act quickly and accept the first hypothesis they produce. These children we call impulsive. Others take a longer time to consider the merits of any hypothesis they generate, oftentimes rejecting an hypothesis they consider to be of poor quality. These children we call reflective. This difference among children is already evident by age six and appears to be consistent within an individual child across problem types and is stable over time (Kagan 1965). This trait becomes part of the child's cognitive style. In addition, younger children, in general, are more impulsive than older children. This aspect of the child's cognitive style should be considered when engaging the child in various academic tasks, including activity-oriented tasks and evaluation tasks. A discussion of this will be expanded in a later chapter.

Problem Solving

According to Yussen and Santrock (1982), four components constitute the process of problem solving. Differences in how children negotiate these components account for the developmental differences in problem solving that are seen. The four components are (a) problem identification; (b) planning the approach to solving the problem; (c) monitoring the progress; and (d) checking the solutions.

Children become better problem solvers as they become more knowledgeable about the world around them, build a repertoire of strategies with which to solve problems, and become more knowledgeable about their own cognitive activity. In the next section, the process in which children construct knowledge and the factors that affect children's ability to construct knowledge is examined. The final section of this chapter discusses the curricular implications related to the developmental differences in children's ability to process information, construct knowledge, and problem solve.

CONSTRUCTING KNOWLEDGE

As stated in Chapter 1, much of what we know about young children's thinking we credit to Piaget. Piaget views human cognition as the biological adaptation of an organism to his or her complex environment. Piaget and his associates view children's construction of knowledge as the interrelationship among four factors: biological maturation; physical experiences in the environment; environmental social experiences; and equilibration (Inhelder, Sinclair, and Bovet 1974). An understanding of how these factors operate and relate to each other provides the foundation for the understanding of how to provide age-appropriate experiences for children, how individual differences are accommodated in the curriculum, which kinds of curriculum materials to provide for children, which kinds of instructional strategies to use with children, and what would be appropriate curriculum content for young children, as well as how to sequence the curriculum experiences.

Biological Maturation

Biological maturation refers to the influence of genetic inheritance on development (Gullo 1985). Piaget explains that children universally progress through stages of cognitive development in exactly the same order. However, it is well established that the rate at which children progress through the stages may vary. One factor that influences the rate of development is the genetic potential of each individual (Phillips 1975). Therefore, the impact of biological maturation on the early childhood curriculum is twofold. First, because of the universal characteristics, there are certain behavioral expectations that are predictable for all five-year-olds, all six-year-olds, and so on. An understanding of these predictable sequences of development makes it possible to provide experiences for children that are age appropriate. Age appropriateness is one of the characteristics of "developmentally appropriate practice" according to the National Association for the Education of Young Children (Bredekamp 1987).

Another characteristic of developmentally appropriate practice is individual appropriateness (Bredekamp 1987). As stated above, although the sequence of development is the same for all children, they progress through these stages at different rates. Therefore, not all children who are the same age can be

20

expected to be exactly at the same place at the same time, either developmentally or academically. An understanding of the normal range of development permits the teacher to create a curriculum and experiences that are flexible and that will meet individual children's needs. Although biological maturation is one factor that affects the rate of development, it cannot be considered in isolation from the kinds of experiences that children have, either physical and social.

Physical Experience

In order to construct knowledge, children must have physical experiences in their environment. Physical experiences include those interactions that children have with the objects and materials that are part of their home and school environments. Piaget and Inhelder (1969) categorize children's physical experiences into two types.

Physical experience proper describes children's interactions through which they discover the properties and nature of objects. For example, a child learns that objects are hard or soft, liquid or solid, breakable or unbreakable, heavy or light, and so on, by manipulating them. By interacting with objects in this manner, children begin to make internalized comparisons of these physical events in their environment.

In logico-mathematical physical experience, children construct knowledge, not from the physical experience itself but rather from reflecting on it. The child learns indirectly that relations that are apparent in one physical experience can also be applied to other experiences. An important aspect of this type of knowledge is that it contains logical rules that can be applied to any objects (Gallagher and Reid 1981). For example, children construct knowledge about objects that are round. They learn that all round objects can roll.

By having both physical experiences proper as well as logico-mathematical physical experiences, children are able to make sense out of their environment by constructing categories of reality. As children "experience" the sand or water table, for example, not only do they come to understand the properties of sand, water, containers, and props, but they also begin to conceptualize the relationships among them. As they "play" with objects in the water, they can group them into "those that float" and "those that sink." They can reconceptualize them into groups that hold the same amount of water or sand (even though they are different shapes). By having these kinds of experiences children learn about concepts such as "more and less," "long and short," "heavy and light," "big and little." They learn about similarities and differences, one-to-one correspondence, and problem solving. It is, in fact, necessary for children to have these kinds of physical experiences before they can go on to such representational skills as reading, writing, and calculating (Bredekamp 1987). Children's early physical, concrete, and nonabstract behavioral structures lay the foundation for later mental structures.

Children come to school having had many physical experiences. It is a misconception to think that some children are environmentally deprived and therefore lack physical experiences before they come to school. It is true that not all children have had the same physical experiences; some, in fact, may not have had the requisite experiences that schools expect from children to ensure success, academically or socially, from the schools' point of view. The kinds of physical experiences that children have are determined both by their biological maturation, as well as by their home and school environments. Children who have an urban experience might have a different understanding of transportation than do children who experience the rural life. Children living on farms would have a different understanding of animals than those children who live in a large apartment complex in the city. Children who lack certain fine-motor ability may not seek out experiences with objects that require extensive fine-motor coordination, while those children who are apparently precocious in this area further develop their fine-motor skills by deliberately engaging themselves in activities that require fine-motor capabilities. Many of the differences we see in children that we attribute to their cultural, linguistic, or socioeconomic backgrounds stem from the different physical experiences provided by those environments.

Children who are at different maturational levels or who have culturally, linguistically, or economically different environmental experiences, will not construct knowledge in the same way, even given the same physical experience. This is why children must be exposed to and allowed to interact with the objects and materials in their physical environment on repeated occasions, and in different contexts, so that they have the opportunity to glean new information from the experience, to learn from their past experiences as well as to learn from others' experiences.

Social Experience

In order to construct knowledge, children must also have social experiences. Social experience is the knowledge that one gains by interaction with people. This includes social relationships, education, language, and culture (Gallagher and Reid 1981). As with maturation, the specific social milieu of particular children may affect the rate at which certain children progress through the stages of cognitive development as well as the nature of the knowledge that is constructed. Social experiences also make it possible for the child's thinking to become more flexible and to understand events from others' points of view.

In the early childhood classroom, social interaction facilitates children's learning and development (Biber 1984; Rogers and Ross 1986; Spodek 1985). When children are encouraged to interact with other children in the early childhood setting, they have opportunities to problem solve, to work out solutions to disputes, and to learn cooperation.

Take, for example, a small group of first graders constructing a cityscape in the block area. While working in a small group, these children must decide what kind of structures will be part of the scene, how tall the structures should be, how many structures should be built, which responsibilities each child has in the project, and how the project will be used upon completion.

An important part of what is gained through social interaction is the feedback that one gets from others, often providing insights into one's own thinking. The major role of the teacher is that of facilitator. The teacher facilitates by providing the appropriate environment for promoting productive social interaction as well as by guiding social interaction by questioning, modeling, and offering suggestions.

Equilibration

Neither maturation nor experience alone (physical or social) can explain the sequential nature of development or the different rates at which development progresses among individual children. It is equilibration that coordinates all other factors (Piaget and Inhelder 1969). Equilibration is a self-regulatory process whereby children constantly adapt to the environment until they reach an internal state of balance or equilibrium. When children enter into a situation where they are confronted with an incongruent or discrepant cognitive experience, they will adapt to it by constructing new knowledge or generalizing existing knowledge to fit the discrepant situation. Equilibration is a self-regulating mechanism whereby the child can determine the rate at which new knowledge will be acquired (Osborn and Osborn 1983).

In the early childhood setting, the environment, both physical and social, should provide a modicum of discrepancy (Seefeldt and Barbour 1990; Spodek 1985). In this manner, children must "stretch" and create new information so that the discrepancy can be resolved.

For example, when we introduce the concept of "magnetism" to children, we generally will provide them with objects on which to test the magnetic property. The first step would be to guide children's thinking so that they could formulate an hypothesis regarding those things that magnets can and cannot pick up. If we gave them the following objects—pins, paper clips, nails, pencils, plastic spoons, and a crayon—the children would probably come to the conclusion that magnets pick up metal things or shiny things. Although this is a correct assumption, it represents an incomplete concept regarding magnetism. Children would never expand their concepts of magnetism as long as all of their experiences justify their hypothesis (equilibrium). Therefore, in order for children to construct new knowledge regarding magnets they must encounter a discrepancy that would thus put them into disequilibrium. How do we facilitate this? By providing experiences for children that violate their hypothesis. So, we could add to their collection of objects a dime, a metal spoon, and a key. All of the physical experiences provided for children must be accompanied with the social experiences of asking them to explain their ideas, questioning their ideas, working with other children to solve a problem, and so forth.

When children come to school they come already having had physical experiences and social experiences, and they are at a particular stage of maturation. As stated earlier, there is no such thing as environmental deprivation. All children have had experiences in an environment. Rather, it is more appropriate to state that there are different types of environments in which children have experiences. These different types of environments may be the result of such factors as culture, language, economic status, family, neighborhood, etc. In early childhood education, it is important to recognize the different types of environmental experiences that children in the classroom have had. The curriculum is then developed, modified, and implemented, based on the individual needs of the children in the classroom.

COGNITIVE CHARACTERISTICS IN EARLY CHILDHOOD

The characteristics of children's problem-solving abilities and cognitive development, in general, change over time as a result of maturation and experiences. However, there are certain aspects of children's thinking during the early childhood years that are characteristic of all children in a particular stage. These constant characteristics of cognitive development during any one stage of development are what Piaget calls cognitive structures (Piaget 1963).

Cognitive structures act as a filter system through which children process information, construct knowledge, and solve problems. The result of having the same cognitive structures at any one particular stage of development is that when children within a stage solve a problem "incorrectly" and give the "wrong answer" to that problem, usually they will all give the same "wrong answer." Children who are in the preoperational stage of development exhibit four cognitive structures that make their thinking qualitatively different from children who are in other stages, yet similar to other children within the preoperational stage. These cognitive structures are *centration, egocentricity, irreversibility of thought, and static thought.* In some ways the preoperational stage of cognitive development is described in negative terms. Young children's thinking in this stage is usually expressed in terms of its limitations, that is, it describes what the child cannot do, rather than what the child can do.

Centration

Centration refers to the preoperational child's tendency to focus his or her attention on one salient or significant perceptual feature of an event or object while not taking into account other relevant features while processing information (Ginsburg and Opper 1978). As a result of centration, the child may have an incomplete understanding of the event or object and solve problems or make judgments based on this partial meaning. Another implication of centration is that the child in this stage can focus on only one aspect of the situation or on one attribute of an object at a time.

One way in which centration manifests itself in the classroom is in the child's ability to judge whether the physical transformation of a continuous quantity is relevant or irrelevant. Whether or not children can make such judgments affects their ability to solve problems related to the resulting amount. This situation usually is found in math or science activities.

For example, take two rows of pennies containing equal numbers of coins. One of the rows is longer than the other because the pennies are more spread out. In a one-to-one correspondence task, the centrating preoperational child might conclude that the longer row of pennies has more than the shorter row even though the space between the pennies in the longer row is greater. In this situation, the child focuses (centrates) his or her attention on the length of the row while he/she disregards the density of the row.

Centration may also affect children's understanding that objects and events can be classified into more than one category. In reading, children eventually have to come to understand that the letter *c* has both the hard *k* sound as well as the soft *s* sound. At the same time, they have to understand that at times *c* and *k* have the same sound and at other times *c* and *s* are equivalents. In math children have to learn that zero is the identity element for addition and subtraction (operating with this digit yields no change in the amount), while in multiplication and division, one is the identity element. Because preoperational children cannot decenter, they have some difficulty solving problems involving transformations, multiple classifications, and operating with factors on multiple levels.

Egocentricity

Egocentricity is related to centration. The term

27

egocentricity is used here not as an indication that the child is selfish and self-centered in the pejorative sense, but rather descriptively to indicate that the child has difficulty in taking another person's point of view or perspective on things (Gullo and Bersani 1983). Egocentricity is related to centration in that the child focuses in, or centrates on his/her *own* point of view or perspective. Preoperational children can display egocentric behavior on either a physical or social level.

Physical egocentricity refers to the child's inability to visually "see" things from a vantage point other than his or her own. The result of this type of behavior may be left/right reversals, not understanding a physical model if the language referring to it reflects another's perspective, or misinterpreting visual information if it is depicted from a vantage point other than that to which the child is accustomed.

Social egocentricity refers to the preoperational child's propensity to consider only the effects of social situations on himself/herself, rather than to take into account how they may also affect others. Take, for example, the four-year-old who pushed another child off his bike during play time, after which the transgressor is made to go into "time-out" to "think" about what he's done. When later asked by the teacher why he shouldn't push other children off their bikes (of course, the hoped for answer would be "because the child might get hurt"), the child replies, "because then I have to go into time-out!"

Children's language is at times idiosyncratic because they are egocentric. They use words that seem to have no logical referents or associations. They often talk about objects and events that are out of context and then become frustrated when they are misunderstood or not understood at all. As discussed earlier, the social experiences that children have are very important for giving them the type of social feedback they require for developing the ability to decenter, both physically and socially.

Irreversibility of Thought

Irreversibility of thought refers to the preoperational child's inability to reverse a process mentally. All mathematical and logical operations are reversible (Phillips 1975). Children who see water poured from one of two identical short, fat glasses with equivalent amounts of water into a tall, thin glass will say that the tall, thin glass has more water (centering on the height of the glass). They are unable to logically solve the problem by mentally reversing the process—thinking that all they would have to do is pour the water back into the short, fat glass and then the amounts would be the same, again; nothing has been added, nothing taken away. Very closely related to irreversible thought is static thought.

Static Thought

Static thought (as opposed to dynamic thought) refers to the child's centrating on the successive states of a transformation, rather than on the *transformation* itself (Osborn and Osborn 1983; Phillips 1975). To go back to the water transformation problem presented above, by focusing on the actual transformation it would be easy to come to the conclusion that the water in the tall glass is the *same* water that was in the short glass. To the preoperational child, it is as though they are observing a series of "still photographs" rather than the "motion picture" that the adult or older child sees. As a result, young children in the preoperational stage of cognitive development have great difficulty in solving problems and understanding events that involve action sequences.

Children whose thinking is characterized by irreversibility of thought and static-thought children require certain kinds of experiences when the activities in which they are engaged involve transformation. First, activities should be chosen that focus on the transformation, the change from one state to another, rather than on the beginning and the end states. Mixing colors focuses on the beginning states (start with two colors) and the end state (end up with a third color), while making butter from cream focuses on the transformation from one state to another to another (start with cream, cream turns into whipped cream, finally into butter). Second, activities should be selected in which the rate of transformation is rapid and observable, such as ice or snow melting into water. Rapid and observable transformations are important for younger children and for children who are acquiring new concepts. Third, it should be noted that some transformations are reversible, while others are not. Again, for younger children and for children in the early stages of acquiring new concepts, it is important to begin by using transformations that are reversible. For example, when introducing the concept of color mixing, if one chooses to mix food coloring into water, this transformation is not reversible. If, however, one mixes colors by looking through colored cellophane toward a light source, this is a reversible transformation.

Because of the characteristics of preoperational thought described above, the thought processes of the preoperational child are often portrayed as "intuitive" rather than "logical," as they will become eventually. It is important to remember that often a child's language will misrepresent what the child really knows. Children will use words and concepts for which they have only partial meaning (Osborn and Osborn 1983). As Piaget states, "Thought always lags behind action and cooperation has to be practiced for a long time before its consequences can be brought fully to light by reflective thought" (Piaget 1955, p. 104).

IMPLICATIONS FOR THE CURRICULUM

One of the most apparent developmental characteristics of children's thinking in the preoperational stage, which consequently has a significant impact on curriculum development, is that children do not develop and learn in compartmentalized ways. For example, in constructing knowledge children do not rely on only one developmental modality (i.e., cognition, language, physical-motor, etc.) in order to make sense out of their world. Rather, they use an integrated set of these modes. Likewise, in processing information, children do not rely solely on perceptual strategies, attention strategies, or memory strategies alone. Again, these strategies are integrated and each affects the other in the child's processing of information. Taking this into account, there are two major implications for the curriculum.

First, the curriculum in early childhood education should reflect an integration of the content areas. An integrated curriculum is one in which each of the parts (content areas such as language/reading, math, social studies, etc.) is recognized for its significance in and of itself, but also is recognized as being a part of a significant whole (Krogh 1990). Teachers who adopt this model, either consciously or unconsciously, view the curriculum holistically, in which a number of individual components are incorporated at one time. This method is often referred to as "webbing" (Krogh 1990), metaphorically referring to the spider's web in which the strength of the entire web is dependent upon the strength of its individual strands.

In addition to integrating the individual content areas to make up the whole, the curriculum is usually constructed around a theme (more will be said about the reasons for this in Chapter 3). According to Krogh (1990), the advantages of the integrated curriculum are (a) that it closely matches the natural ways in which children learn spontaneously in their environment; (b) it provides for greater depth of curriculum coverage; (c) it builds upon children's natural interests; (d) it teaches children knowledge, processes, and skills in a meaningful context; (e) it provides for maximum flexibility with the curriculum; and (f) it provides teachers with a curriculum-planning device.

Having an integrated approach does not mean that when you open the teacher's plan book you see nothing written there except integrated curriculum. Rather, it means that when the teacher is planning math activities, for example, he or she is aware that certain language skills and concepts are perhaps prerequisites for the mathematical concepts that are the focus of the particular activity. Likewise, when planning social studies activities or any other content area activities, the teacher is aware what other curriculum area concepts and skills are woven into the activity. In an integrated approach, it is important to approach teaching with the mind-set that one does not isolate the curriculum areas with the expectancy that only math or social studies is being taught within any one activity.

As an example of an activity that might serve to exemplify an integrated approach, have children classify food items into the categories of fruits and vegetables as part of a "food" theme. In order to do this, you might use a floor graph. A floor graph is a two- or three-column graph that is created on the floor of the classroom with masking tape or other types of tape. It is usually left there so that it can be used in different ways or used by the children whenever they so desire. At the top of one of the columns the word *Fruit* is written along with the picture of an apple as a symbol for fruit. At the top of the other column, *Vegetable* is written, along with a picture of a carrot. Each child is then provided with a fruit or a vegetable (either a picture or the actual item). When called on, each child, in turn, places his or her item in a box under the appropriate column and a short discussion of each of the items takes place. This discussion might include the label, how it tastes, how it grows, how one knows whether it's a fruit or a vegetable, and so on. After each child has placed his or her item or picture on the graph, the following questions might be posed: "How many fruits are there on the graph?" "How many vegetables are there on the graph?" "Are there more fruits or vegetables on the graph?" "How many more?" "How many fruits and vegetables are there altogether?"

In this one activity, science concepts (fruits, vegetables, health, how things grow); social studies concepts (where things grow); language/reading concepts (vocabulary, symbols, discussion); and math concepts (counting, more, less, total) are directly addressed. In addition, children have been asked to think, to problem solve, to use language, and to be involved physically in the activity.

Second, because children don't learn and develop in a compartmentalized manner, an integration of developmental skills used for learning within the early childhood setting should be accommodated for in the curriculum (Gullo 1989; Krogh 1990; McGarry 1986). Children learn best if they have an opportunity to *know* something in a variety of ways. Children can learn information through repetition; however, they need to experience the knowledge within a variety of contexts and through using various developmental domains. Children should be given opportunities in the curriculum to *know* through language, through thinking and problem solving, through touching, through affect, through seeing, and through hearing.

How can a curriculum, which takes into account the ways children learn and develop, be implemented? Through carefully planned experiences within an environment that facilitates learning and development. Chapter 3 considers the characteristics of the classroom environment and strategies for implementing the curriculum within this environment.

Chapter 3

CREATE A CLASSROOM ENVIRONMENT THAT FACILITATES LEARNING AND DEVELOPMENT

The early childhood environment is the stage upon which the players, props, sets, and situations all work together to enhance and facilitate learning and development in young children. The script is the curriculum and it is written and directed to ensure that everyone has a part written specifically for him or her. All of the endings are happy!

An effective early childhood environment is one in which the child's learning and development is sustained in many ways. It is an environment that provides choices for children within a structure specifically designed to enhance and support the curriculum. It is an environment that provides for children's interactions with objects and with other children and adults. It is an environment that maintains children's interests, and provides experiences that are meaningful and interesting. It is an environment that is responsive to individual children's needs by providing flexibility in the curriculum.

In this chapter, a number of factors related to the early childhood environment are discussed. Research related to effective environments, and examples of how to apply this knowledge to the implementation of the curriculum are presented.

OBJECTS IN THE ENVIRONMENT

Objects in the environment refer to the materials with which children interact in order to process information, construct knowledge, and solve problems. Taking into account the developmental nature of the child during the early childhood years, these materials should have certain characteristics.

First, the materials should be real or concrete whenever possible (Kamii 1985; Schickendanz 1986). This is particularly important for children in the earlier part of preoperations, or for children who are being instructed in new concepts and therefore are being asked to construct new knowledge, as opposed to using existing knowledge in new ways. Real objects contain information for children that pretend objects or pictures of objects simply don't have. As stated in Chapter 2, children rely on perceptual information when they construct knowledge; therefore, real and concrete objects and materials in the early childhood environment support this manner of learning.

Consider, for a moment, the integrated activity discussed previously involving the categorization of fruits and vegetables. What kinds of information could a child get from a "real" orange in contrast to a "pretend" orange, or to a picture of an orange, or to being told about an orange. Imagine that you are holding a real orange in one hand and a plastic model of an orange in the other. What's the first thing that you notice? Well, the two oranges have discernibly different weights. Also, if you apply pressure to the two oranges, you will be able to tell something about their consistency. Rub your thumb over the two oranges. The textures are different and one of the oranges leaves an oily residue on your thumb. Look carefully at the two oranges. The color of one of the oranges is consistent, the other might have color variations across its skin. Bring first one orange and then the other to your nose. Notice any difference? The differences suggested here are noticeable simply by holding the oranges. Only one of the oranges can be peeled, taken apart, squeezed into juice, and eaten. Children need experiences with real objects in order to make sense out of their world and construct new knowledge.

A second characteristic of the objects or materials from which children learn is that they be manipulatives (Kamii 1985). Children must have experiences with real objects that they can manipulate before they are able to understand the meaning of symbols such as numbers and letters. Children must have opportunities to experiment with objects in such ways as putting them into piles or groups, pouring from them, stacking them, using them representationally, and simply interacting with them in conjunction with other children and adults. While the ability to accept and use symbols is important for every area of the curriculum, the use of manipulatives to prepare children for the abstract use of representational symbols in early childhood education is epitomized in the current wave of mathematics programs available for the early childhood classroom. Two of these programs, "Mathematics Their Way" (Baratta-Lorton 1976) and "Explorations" (Harcourt 1988) represent comprehensive prekindergarten through third grade curricula in which manipulatives are the bases for teaching a wide range of knowledge, processes, operations, and skills. The theoretical underpinnings of both of these curricula is that only through the manipulation of and interaction of objects coupled with meaningful social and language experiences can children come to understand abstraction and accept the symbols attached to these abstractions.

The third important characteristic of objects in the child's environment is that they be relevant to the life experiences of children (Biber 1984; Forman and Kuschner 1983). As discussed previously, children who are in the preoperational stage of cognitive development are both egocentric and centrate on the salient perceptual aspects of objects or situations. Because of these characteristics, it is important that teachers take into account children's previous experiences in making decisions relative to the types of physical experiences and objects that will be incorporated into the curriculum. In order to be meaningful, the objects used in the physical experiences that children have must be relevant to their life experiences.

Once again, let's return to the fruit and vegetable integrated activity that was presented earlier. If the objective of the activity is to have children categorize fruits and vegetables and in the process acquire knowledge relative to the discriminate attributes that differentiate between fruits and vegetables, then it is important to use only those fruits and vegetables that are known to the children who make up the class. If, on the other hand, the objective of the activity is to have children generalize what they've learned regarding differentiating fruits and vegetables, then it might be appropriate to introduce items that are out of the children's experiential realm. By having physical experiences with objects that are relevant and familiar to them, the children might hypothesize that fruits are sweet, have juice, and have seeds, while vegetables don't have seeds, may grow under the ground, or are actually the leaves or the stems of plants. At that time, if a fruit that is not relevant to children's experiences is introduced, the children could draw on past experiences and generalize the information in order to categorize the unfamiliar object as a fruit or vegetable. While the definition that the children have developed regarding what makes a fruit a fruit and a vegetable a vegetable is somewhat incomplete, it nonetheless will be helpful to them in making informed decisions about new experiences. Children who live in warm climates might have difficulty understanding the concepts in an activity if it involves snow or ice, while children who do not live near an ocean might have difficulty understanding that salt occurs in water naturally and that water comes into the shore and goes out again every day. While certain concepts are difficult to comprehend for some children, they are not difficult to comprehend for others, even though they are the same age, if these concepts are relevant to their everyday experiences.

INTERACTION IN THE ENVIRONMENT

We know from Chapter 2 that young children learn best in an environment that encourages interaction. Children interact not only with objects in their environment, they also interact with other children and with adults in their environment. Through interaction, children construct knowledge and learn to problem solve. The early childhood classroom should be one that is designed to facilitate social interaction (Gullo 1988a; Rogers and Ross 1986). Too often the classroom is the place where quality is judged by how quiet it is rather than by how much activity is taking place. It should be noted that in early childhood education, the term "lesson" has been relinquished for the more appropriate term "activity." It is through activities that young children learn most efficaciously. It should be noted also that the root word in activity is *active,* which describes the manner that best facilitates learning in young children. It is not until children are older, about seven or eight (Bredekamp 1987), that they will begin to benefit from some teacher lecture-oriented lessons.

Play is the primary activity through which social interaction is facilitated most often in the early childhood classroom. Examination of the definition of play reveals that this activity meets the criteria for facilitating the construction of knowledge and acquiring new skills. According to Garvey (1977), play has the following characteristics:

1. Play has intrinsic motivation. Children play as a result of some inner drive and not from external pressures. Activities are pursued for their own sake or for reasons determined by the individual.

2. Play is enjoyable. The child takes pleasure in the activity, though the outward manifestation of this pleasure can vary.

3. Play is flexible and free from externally imposed rules. It varies from situation to situation and from person to person.

4. Play is nonliteral. It requires players to realize that what is happening is not what seems to be happening. In play children are not bound by reality, but act as if the events were real or exhibit a "what-if" attitude regarding the situation.

5. Play requires verbal, mental, or physical activity. Lounging, though perhaps pleasurable, is not active and thus does not fit into a definition of play (Garvey 1977, p. 4).

In the early childhood classroom setting, there should be

opportunities for young children to be engaged in learning activities with other children as well as with the teacher. This can best be accomplished in small groups. Through interaction with others, a number of things are accomplished.

Through social interaction, children are exposed to other children's points of view. Because children of early childhood age are egocentric, it is important that they have opportunities to work together toward a common goal. In this way, they will have the chance to make decisions based on compromise and common agreement. These opportunities help children decenter from their own perspectives and begin to value that there is more than one way of doing something.

Through social interaction in the classroom, children have the opportunity to experience cooperation. Fostering a sense of cooperation rather than a feeling of competition is essential in early childhood education.

Experiencing cooperation in the classroom can be accomplished on two levels. First, cooperation will occur spontaneously, but only if children are allowed to interact socially over extended periods of the day and if the environment provides the necessary props and activities. Second, cooperation will occur on a more formal level if the teacher implements some of the learning activities by using cooperative learning methods. In this method children are grouped heterogeneously in small groups to complete an activity. This can be accomplished with all the age groups represented within early childhood parameters. For instance, in the prekindergarten or kindergarten classroom, children could be grouped together to create a mural or construction out of assorted materials. If the theme is provided to the children, along with adult suggestions, this goal is not unrealistic. In the second or third grade, children may work cooperatively on a science project such as putting together some type of collection that corresponds with the science theme being studied.

Finally, social interaction increases children's metacognitive awareness. Metacognition is being aware of your own thinking (Markman 1977). For early childhood, the implications of metacognitive awareness manifest themselves in understanding when you don't understand something or in the awareness that your understanding of something differs from someone else's. Often, children who are in the preoperational stage of development don't know when they don't understand a problem or a situation. Perhaps this is why, when we ask a group of first graders whether they have any questions regarding instructions or about an activity we are preparing to do, they seldom have any. Yet, when they are engaged in the activity it becomes apparent that not all of the children understood what they were to do. It is not until we are engaged in social interaction does feedback from others become possible. Feedback provides insights into one's own thinking by way of the questions and reactions of others. It is also through social interaction that we can get insights into how others are thinking, both through their actions and language.

Social interaction should be encouraged and planned for in the classroom environment. This is best achieved by presenting children with learning activities that promote action, interaction, and reaction.

LEARNING CONTEXTS IN THE ENVIRONMENT

The early childhood classroom environment provides many different contexts in which children have opportunities to process, construct, and demonstrate knowledge. These contexts include opportunities for learning socially, physically, emotionally, linguistically, perceptually, concretely, representationally, and abstractly. As stated earlier, preoperational children exhibit centration; that is, they often focus on particular perceptual attributes or characteristics of a situation when they are trying to understand it. As a result, children's understanding of a concept, word, or representational process is often context specific; they can only demonstrate understanding if the concept, word, or

41

representational process is presented in precisely the same manner and in exactly the same context in which they learned it.

Take, for example, the first grader who is learning to print using the D'Nealian method. In this method, the letters have somewhat different combinations of straight and curved lines as compared to the Palmer technique of printing. Children learn the names of the letters by associating the name with the shape of the letter, in much the same way as they learn the names of objects. Some children, who learn the names of letters using only one method of letter formation, may have difficulty recognizing the letter when it is made using another method. The same thing can be seen in early readers. They often have difficulty recognizing a familiar word when it is written in a script other than the one they are used to such as italics or fancy script.

This phenomenon can be explained developmentally. Piaget (1963) states that children do not demonstrate consistent competencies in their behaviors because they are "not at the same level" in their development for all skills, concepts, or other types of abilities. The French word for this is *decalage*. The type of decalage exhibited here is called "vertical decalage." Vertical decalage refers to the child's having to restructure formally acquired knowledge at a later time (Ginsburg and Opper 1978). For example, a child may "fail" a problem when it is presented to him or her on a verbal or symbolic (pictorial or written) level, while he/she is quite capable of solving the same problem behaviorally or in a pragmatic context. This illustrates that there are different ways of "knowing," and because a child demonstrates "knowing" in one way, it does not mean that he or she can generalize the knowledge to all contexts.

Another illustration of this phenomenon can be found in a common early childhood learning objective for prekindergarten and kindergarten—the learning of colors, shapes, and sizes. When the teacher attempts to assess whether the child has acquired a color concept, he/she generally asks the child to identify particular colors in one way or another by responding to the color label. If the child cannot respond appropriately, the

42

assumption is that the child does not have the particular color concept. For example, when the teacher asks the child, "Give me the red ball," or "What color is this ball?" and the child doesn't respond or responds inappropriately, the teacher assumes that the child does not have the concept red. In the above scenario, the child is being asked to match a particular perceptual attribute with a verbal label. This is very different than if the teacher asks, "Give me a ball that is the same color as this one" (holding another red ball), or (holding a red ball and a green ball) "Are these two balls the same color?" In the first scenario the teacher is judging the child's conceptual or perceptual knowledge via his/her verbal performance or knowledge. The added verbal performance requirement is removed from the second scenario and success is more likely. If the child can respond appropriately to the second type of questions, but not to the first, it may be that the child has the conceptual knowledge but not the verbal performance or label that accompanies it. We cannot assume that failure at one level means that the child does not have the concept, and conversely, that success at one level is an indication that the child comprehends completely.

Children need repeated experiences in order to process information and construct knowledge about a specific concept or process (Ginsburg and Opper 1978; Gullo 1989; Phillips 1975). However, drill and practice in only one context will yield limited understanding. Using flash cards only, for example, to teach children numbers, letters, and so on, will mean that they may have difficulty in recognizing or using them meaningfully in dissimilar contexts (Kamii 1985). Likewise, if children learn number concepts and operations using only manipulatives and never have opportunities for associating them with representational images, they too will have difficulty when it comes to paper and pencil tasks. Therefore, practice using paper and pencil activities may be appropriate even when the initial acquisition of the concept requires hands-on concrete experiences. The solution is a balance of the types of activities available for children in the environment so that they have opportunities to acquire knowledge and demonstrate knowledge at various levels and in various contexts.

INDIVIDUALIZING THROUGH THE ENVIRONMENT

Children in early childhood education classrooms today represent a vastly more heterogeneous group than the children of even a decade ago (Gullo 1990a). The educational needs of contemporary children therefore are more varied. Environmental as well as developmental disparities among young children in the early childhood classrooms have resulted in the need to respond more to the individual needs of these children. Children enter school having had different types of prekindergarten experiences, ranging from none at all to one with highly academic foci. Children enter school with vastly different cultural and linguistic experiences. Children enter school from different socioeconomic backgrounds and family structures. Children who enter school represent a much wider age-range within grade level. These factors alone, and in conjunction with each other, make it necessary to individualize the curriculum to some extent in order to meet the needs of today's children. The manner in which the classroom environment is designed and utilized represents the primary means through which the early childhood curriculum can be individualized. The chief way in which the environment can accommodate individual children's educational needs is through the use of *activity centers.*

Activity centers are areas in the learning environment that are specified according to curriculum content areas, concepts, skills, or knowledge. Day and Drake (1983) state that the experiences in the activity centers may be adapted according to the individual child's interests, prior experiences or knowledge, level of maturity, or learning style. In this way, an activity center approach offers an individualized approach to instruction in the early childhood classroom.

An activity center approach is appropriate for the entire grade level range of early childhood education. It is designed to be an environment in which children have opportunities to manipulate materials, to engage in social interaction through conversation, dramatic role playing, and cooperative learning episodes, as well as to learn at their own level and pace. Activity centers emphasize cognitive growth and provide for self-evaluation (Leeper 1974). In addition, a center approach provides children with opportunities for constructing new knowledge and acquiring new skills, reinforcing and practicing existing knowledge and skills as well as providing the medium through which the curriculum content areas can be integrated. According to Day and Drake (1983), children develop independent learning skills and acquire as well as enhance existing knowledge and skills to provide the foundation on which new knowledge can be constructed and new skills acquired.

In prekindergarten and kindergarten, activity centers are usually organized according to the type of activity that occurs there. Examples of prekindergarten or kindergarten centers might be creative arts, blocks, dramatic play, manipulatives, music, library, audiovisual, and inquiry. In the early primary grades the centers are more aligned with the subject areas of the curriculum. Activity centers in the primary grades might include mathematics, language arts, social studies, and science. In addition, the primary classroom might also contain a number of the centers found in the prekindergarten and kindergarten rooms as well.

Day and Drake (1983) outline a number of conditions that should be met if activity centers are to be effective in the early childhood classroom:

1. An effective management system must be developed and well understood by the teacher and children.

2. The teacher must genuinely know the children and their abilities, achievement levels, previous experiences, and

overall maturity (physical, mental, emotional). In addition, he or she must know the goals and objectives of a good early childhood program and apply these goals in designing the curriculum.

3. The centers must be attractive and well organized, provide for a variety of learning styles and skill levels, include necessary supplies and resources, and provide for feedback through self-correcting materials of various types.

4. Children must be taught how to effectively use the center materials and equipment.

5. Individual and group planning guidance, and evaluation of center activities must be provided.

6. The children must possess the necessary skills and prerequisite information for effective utilization of the centers. They must understand the purposes of their activities; be able to exercise self-discipline; and depending on their reading or computational level, be able to keep good records of their activities.

7. The activities in the centers should have educationally valid purposes. They should reinforce skills, concepts, and knowledge; be integrated with other appropriate skills and concepts; and be based on diagnosis of the strengths, weaknesses, and needs of the children. (Day and Drake 1983, p. 14)

In addition to centers meeting the above-listed conditions, the following criteria should also be addressed. Centers should be self-selected by the child, within the structure provided by the teacher and should be changed frequently, so that children's interest levels are maintained. It may be necessary to change some centers on a daily basis so that the integrity of the unit themes is preserved.

CHARACTERISTICS OF THE LEARNING ENVIRONMENT

The early childhood learning environment should be one that is dynamic (changing to meet the needs of children) rather than static (unchanging and standardized or overly structured). Five dimensions have been identified by Jones (n.d.) that may be used to analyze the physical environment, both materials as well as setting. These dimensions include:

Soft _____ hard
Open _____ closed
Simple _____ complex
Intrusion _____ seclusion
High mobility _____ low mobility

Soft settings are provided for comfort, where small groups of children or individual children can go to read or talk quietly. These settings might include rugs, pillows, a soft easy chair, bean bag chairs, or a couch. Hard settings, such as the floor, table tops, work benches, and counter tops are available to withstand the kinds of activities that children might engage in at a more vigorous level. Soft instructional materials might include clay, play dough, sand, and various art materials such as cotton, sponges, and fabrics. Hard materials are such things as puzzles, blocks, certain manipulatives, and props.

By having materials available on open shelves that are easily accessed, individual choice by children is facilitated. Children will have to rely on the teacher for access to materials that are on closed shelves, in hard-to-reach places. A balance between the two types of areas best serves the goals of the early childhood curriculum.

Open materials are those that are divergent in nature. The child is not constrained in using the material by the material itself. One example of an open material is playdough. There are many uses one can create for playdough; for example, the child can create many "art" objects with playdough. In addition, playdough could be used in conjunction with math activities by making small balls out of it and using them as manipulatives. In the dramatic play area, children can fashion food out of playdough and use it in conjunction with their play theme. One could see whether it can sink or float at the water table, one could mix red and yellow playdough to see what color it makes, one could make objects to be carried by trucks in the block area—the uses are endless. With closed materials, children are constrained in using them by the material itself, they are convergent in nature. Puzzles are an example of a closed material. With closed materials, there is usually a specific or narrow curriculum objective that may be met by using them. Again, a balance between open and closed materials is most efficacious.

Both simple and complex materials should be provided. Simple materials are those that involve few parts or variables; complex materials are those that include many subparts or many variables. As children progress, simple materials can be made more complex by adding parts or variables. For example, as children increase in their ability to put together simple puzzles, puzzles with more and smaller pieces are made available to them. As children become more adept at creating structures with building materials, props are provided to make the activity more complex. By providing access to both simple and complex materials, and opportunities to engage in both simple as well as complex activities, the needs of children working at different levels are met and individual children are allowed to progress at their own pace. It should be noted, however, if complex materials are presented before the child is developmentally ready, it may result in frustration for the child and the loss of further interest.

As was stated earlier, children should be given opportunities for learning in small groups and in larger groups, as well as individually. Therefore, materials and space should allow for both intrusion as well as seclusion. Open spaces in the room, where children can effectively engage in activities in groups, best facilitates intrusionary activities. In addition, a small table where four children can sit together and work cooperatively on an activity or play a game is also an example of intrusion. Some areas of the room need to be separated from the rest of the room so that a child may work quietly, either individually or with one other child or the teacher. These areas allow for the seclusion of one or two individuals, away from the distraction from the rest of the activity in the room.

Finally, there should be areas in the early childhood learning environment that allow for both high-mobility as well as low-mobility activities. Ideally this should occur in both indoor as well as outdoor spaces.

The focus of this chapter and of Chapter 2 has been primarily on the development of curriculum appropriate for children in the preoperational stage of cognitive development. Much of the discussion concentrated on how it is necessary to take into account children's developmental characteristics when designing the curriculum framework, curriculum activities, and curriculum implementation strategies.

It was suggested that a curriculum that took into account these developmental considerations would be one that would be thematically based, involved activity centers, integrated the curriculum areas, and facilitated individualization through its flexibility. The Appendix provides an example of a two-week kindergarten unit that illustrates the considerations outlined above. Included in this unit is an example of a parent letter that might be used to introduce the unit to the parents.

Chapter 4

CONTINUITY OF CHILD DEVELOPMENT AND THE IMPLICATIONS FOR TEACHING PRACTICE

At the heart of a developmentally appropriate early childhood curriculum are the concepts of "age appropriateness" and "individual appropriateness" (Bredekamp 1987). These two curriculum constructs recognize that while there are similarities within an age group of children, there are also individual differences within the group of children and within the child himself/herself.

There are two types of individual differences that must be taken into account when planning for children. First, there are the interpersonal individual differences. These are the types of differences that we see in school and in other performance between children because of differences in rates of maturation or in the types of prior social and physical experiences they have had. It is manifested in children of the same age by their not being at the same level of understanding or by their not exhibiting the same types of developmental behaviors.

For example, consider two entering first graders. One of these six-year-olds may be to the point where he/she is starting to decenter in his/her thinking. He/she may be able to do multiple classifications (understand that an object can belong to more than one category at a time). In addition, this six-year-old has had countless experiences with books and other forms of print, both at school and at home. This six-year-old also exhibits some advanced fine-motor ability. Contrast this with other the six-year-old, who has had limited exposure to print other than at school, has difficulty cutting with a scissors, and still exhibits centration in his/her thinking. However, this other six-year-old

51

is still within normal limits in all of his/her behaviors. Given these two children, which child would you believe is more ready to read (in the conventional manner)? Of course, the first six-year-old would be. This does not mean that in the end, the two children will not be exhibiting behaviors of a similar developmental level; it simply means that because of certain factors (both biological and experiential), these two children exhibit differences at the present time.

The second type of individual difference to be considered is the intrapersonal individual difference. These are the developmental differences that manifest themselves within an individual. Decalage, one type of which was discussed earlier (Chapter 3), best describes this type of individual difference. As will be recalled, vertical decalage refers to the child's having to restructure formally acquired knowledge at a later time (Ginsburg and Opper 1978). Thus, children may exhibit a difference in their ability to demonstrate knowledge in different contexts, or when different developmental demands are placed on them.

Horizontal decalage is the other type of decalage that explains intrapersonal individual difference. Horizontal decalage refers to the child demonstrating different levels of achievement, knowledge, or understanding with regard to problems involving similar mental operations. This implies that children's development is continuous. That is, they do not exhibit characteristics of one stage on one day, and then of another stage on another day. Children's development is gradual and will exhibit characteristics of more than one stage at a time.

Taken more broadly, age and individual appropriateness have implications not only for within age considerations but for within developmental stage considerations as well. Within the stage of preoperations, children will progress at different rates, exhibit characteristics in common, and demonstrate behaviors indicative of more than one level of the preoperational stage at the same time. For teaching practice, there are three salient implications.

First, recognize and plan for the continuity of development within the curriculum for ages five to eight. We need to view the curriculum as a continuous experience from kindergarten to second or third grade. Teachers at the various grade levels within early childhood should work together to ensure that the experiences from one grade level complement experiences in the other grade levels. In some cases, an integrated kindergarten through grade two or three experience best serves the needs of children at this developmental level.

Second, recognize that there are similarities in patterns of thinking and in the strategies used to construct knowledge in children in the preoperational stage of development. As such, the methods used to teach, the type of content, the types of materials, and the physical environment supporting children's learning at this stage should be more similar than dissimilar. Said differently, children between the ages of five and eight are more alike in what they require for learning than they are different. There is nothing magic about the three months that elapse between the kindergarten and first-grade year that suggests that children's learning experiences should be vastly different. Yet when one walks into most first-grade classrooms, you will find that there is more similarity between the first-grade room and the sixth-grade room than there is between the first grade and kindergarten rooms. This is simply not supported by what we know about how children at this age learn (Bredekamp 1987).

Third, and finally, recognize that by the age of eight, many of the developmental differences that are apparent earlier no longer exist (Elkind 1990). As has been suggested earlier, the individual differences that are seen in the preoperational stage of development are the result of a combination of biological and experiential factors. The end result of this is that there are sometimes vast differences in children's behaviors during this period. Research shows that by the end of the preoperational period, or around age eight, these differences seem to even themselves out, given an environment facilitative of the developmental needs of these children (Anastasiow 1986; Elkind

1990). It is imperative, therefore, not to be hasty in making judgments relative to children's ability levels, particularly in prekindergarten, kindergarten, and first grade. Some children acquire knowledge and/or skills more rapidly than others, but then slow down in their acquisition as time progresses. Other children acquire the same knowledge and/or skills at a more even pace. The end result is that by the end of a given period, these children will be at the same level. The most dangerous implication of this is to judge too early an individual child's potential, when the difference between this child and others may be casused by differences in maturational rate or experiential backgrounds. Conversely, time alone will not be sufficient to ensure that a child will reach his/her developmental potential (Gullo in press; Gullo and Burton in press).

THE GIFT OF TIME

The field of early childhood education has long been associated with the giving of gifts to the young children whom it serves. The first mention of gifts in early childhood education came when Froebel suggested that "gifts" provide the basis of the curriculum in kindergarten. In Froebel's view, the kindergarten curriculum should be balanced between individual children's freedom to engage in self-selected activities and society's responsibility to meet the individual needs of children in order to further the development of appropriate skills, knowledge, and values (Broman 1989). Froebel's gifts were at the heart of his proposed kindergarten curriculum, providing materials such as colored balls of yarn, cubes, cylinders, and spheres to facilitate each child's interactions with actual objects (Morrison 1988). Even by today's standards, Froebel's gifts met all of the key characteristics of developmentally appropriate practice. They were real, concrete, manipulatable, and relevant to the lives of children. Most important, they provided a vehicle for an individualized curriculum (Bredekamp 1987).

54

Recently, yet another gift has been put forward as a central aspect of early childhood education. This new gift, called the "gift of time" (Uphoff and Gilmore 1986) is also to be proffered to kindergarten children. However, here the resemblance to the types of gifts Froebel advocated ends. The gift of time provides no basis for an individualized curriculum. Instead, it actually bears the possibility of diminishing the fundamental purpose of the kindergarten—that is, meeting the individual needs of children.

Nonetheless, the gift of time is the essence of a stance on kindergarten education currently being espoused by Uphoff and Gilmore (1986) among others, which will subsequently affect the later early childhood grade levels. It likewise has become a popular concept among parents owing to its intuitive appeal and to widespread coverage in the popular press (e.g., Kaercher 1984; Weaver 1985). A central assumption of the gift of time perspective is that children in school, particularly those in kindergarten, should be grouped developmentally rather than by chronological age. Thus, if a child is of legal school entry age but tests at a younger developmental age, that child presumably should be given the gift of time, or another year, to become ready for the kindergarten curriculum. According to gift of time advocates, this is the notion of a developmental curriculum.

Clearly, then, there is a fundamental difference between a developmentally appropriate curriculum from a gift of time viewpoint and that of the more commonly accepted view of the National Association for the Education of Young Children (NAEYC: Bredekamp 1987). This fundamental difference pertains specifically to the nature of the relationship among the child, the curriculum, and evaluation. Uphoff and Gilmore (1986) submit that children should be evaluated to ascertain their developmental level and hence, to determine whether they will "fit" into the predetermined kindergarten curriculum—predeterminally set to a specific developmental level. As such, the gift of time proponents view developmentally appropriate practice from the curriculum's perspective. Developmentally appropriate practice occurs if the child developmentally fits the curriculum.

According to NAEYC, on the other hand, children are evaluated in order to determine curricular needs (Bredekamp 1987). The curriculum is adjusted to meet each child's unique needs, ideally achieving a balance between age appropriateness and individual appropriateness. Based on this point of view, developmentally appropriate practice is defined from the child's perspective. Developmentally appropriate practice occurs if the curriculum meets the needs of the children.

Chapter 5

THE ROLE OF PARENT INVOLVEMENT IN THE EARLY CHILDHOOD CURRICULUM

The field of early childhood education has long recognized that the parent is the child's first and most significant teacher. Parents have taken part in the early childhood classroom by providing many varied and important functions. Parents have assisted in field trips, in classroom parties, in making snacks, in making learning materials, in planning special events, in working with small groups in the classroom, and in many, many more ways. Another important role of the parent has been that of policy maker. Parents have participated in many educationally important policy-making roles, particularly in early childhood.

Today, for many reasons, there is a revival of interest in the role that parents play in their children's educational process. The changing family context has been cited as one of the most influential factors (Gullo 1990a; Powell 1989). Changes in contemporary family contexts include, but are not limited to, an increase in the maternal workforce, an increase in single-parent households, a decrease in the number of extended families, and an increase in families seeking programs outside of the traditional academic schooling environment for their children to participate in during nonschool hours.

Recently, however, there has been concern that discontinuity exists between the family home setting and the nonfamilial school setting (Powell 1989). It is suggested that this discontinuity may have negative effects on children. Sources of the child's experience of discontinuity include: differing parent and teacher roles (Katz 1980), different family and school expectations of the child's past experience (Filmore 1988), and different teacher and parent goals for children (Hess, Price, Dickson, and Conroy 1981).

TYPES OF PARENT INVOLVEMENT

According to Epstein (1989), there are five types of parent involvement. These various types of involvement increase home–school partnerships and have the potential of reducing the discontinuity that exists for the child between the expectations of home and the expectations of school.

The first type of parent involvement has as its function to assist families in their parenting roles and to help them to become more effective in their child-rearing. This involves developing programs to increase parents' understanding of basic child development and increasing their ability to establish a more supportive home environment for learning. This could be accomplished through providing parents with opportunities to hear presentations from child development experts, to see films about child development and child-rearing, through providing parents with literature on issues related to child development and parenting, as well as through providing parents with newsletters about what is going on in the curriculum, with suggestions as to how their child's learning experiences could be enhanced at home. In some schools, teachers actually provide parents with learning packets that can be checked out of the classroom. These packets contain the activity objectives, instructions on implementing the activity and materials, or instructions on gathering the materials if they involve common, found-in-the-home objects.

The purpose of the second type of parent involvement is to improve communication between home and school. This can be accomplished by sending home memos or class newsletters on a regular basis. These letters might include information about upcoming events, current curriculum topics and activities, or requests for assistance. It is particularly important to communicate to parents about curriculum methods or materials, the purpose of which might not be familiar to them.

For example, if you are using a whole-language approach to language and reading, in which the children "write" stories using invented or phonetic spelling, it is important that parents be informed about this procedure, its process and purpose. With no communication home about this method, parents might wonder why their children are not bringing home worksheets, or are bringing home stories with misspelled words. A simple explanation from the teacher not only avoids a potential confrontational situation, but also garners the needed support from the home.

Another way in which communication between school and home can be facilitated, particularly in schools where children are dropped off by their parents, is to have a parent bulletin board. This bulletin board is always available and could be maintained by a parent; on it could be information for parents in the form of interesting articles, school information, a school calendar, etc. The bulletin board also could have a section for parents to post information for other parents or notes for the teacher.

The third type of parent involvement involves recruiting and training parents to be volunteers in the classroom or school. The primary purpose of this type of involvement is to support the children's activities and programs. Morrison (1978), lists the following five different functions that parents perform as volunteers, with examples of roles that each might perform.

1. Innovator: Create learning materials;
   Create bulletin boards;
   Create learning centers.

2. Teacher: Provide instruction to groups or individuals;
   Tutor small groups or individuals.

3. Supervisor: Assist in playground supervision;
   Assist with lunch duty;

Assist with field trips;
Assist in classroom supervision;
Assist in extracurricular activities.

4. Clerical: Assist in grading papers;
Assist in recording grades;
Assist in filling out records and forms.

5. Maintainer: Assist in maintaining classroom materials such as library books, learning center activities, or learning files.

Morrison (1978) underscores the importance of training parents if they are to be asked to volunteer in the classroom. It has been found that when parents are brought into the classroom with little or no systematic training, it is less likely that they will continue. Morrison states that the training of parent volunteers is as important as the decision to have volunteer parents in the classroom or school, itself.

The fourth type of parent involvement that Epstein lists is to provide parents with examples of, or ideas for, learning activities at home. In addition to providing the type of learning activity described in the first type of parent involvement discussed, parents could also be provided with curriculum objectives and descriptions of school learning programs. Accompanying this information might be examples of, or guidance in, developing materials and activities at home that would enhance children's school experiences.

The fifth type of parent involvement is to assist parents in developing and establishing leadership roles in schools. This could be accomplished by making parents aware of the various home-school organizations available to them and encouraging them to participate. It is also imperative to make parents aware of their importance in contributing to the school decision-making process, where appropriate.

BENEFITS OF PARENT INVOLVEMENT

Effective parent involvement yields many benefits. Aside from the obvious ones for the teacher, child, and parent, there are some other benefits that are realized at both long- and short-term levels.

Research on parent involvement has demonstrated that there are some differences between parents who are involved and those who are not. Parents who are more involved in their children's education during early childhood demonstrate increased sensitivity to their children's developmental needs; a greater acceptance of their children's behaviors and emotions in general; increased ability to recognize and respect individual differences in their and others' children; and increased communication with their children through reasoning and encouragement rather than through authority (Morrison 1978). More recently, information on parent involvement has shown that it affects parents in ways other than those directly related to parenting knowledge, child development knowledge, schooling, and parenting skills. Research among Head Start parents has shown that parents who are more involved in their child's education during Head Start are more likely to (1) increase their educational level, (2) increase their economic opportunity through increasing job skills, and (3) increase their economic self-sufficiency, in general (Oyemade, Washington, and Gullo 1989).

OBSTACLES TO PARENT INVOLVEMENT

While it has been shown that there are differences in parents' behaviors relative to their participation in their children's education, these differences ultimately affect their children. Children whose parents are involved in their education in early childhood are more likely to demonstrate the following long- and short-term differences, as compared to children whose parents are not involved. Children whose parents are involved are

61

more aware and more responsive to their physical and social environment; they demonstrate better skills for problem solving; they show increased long- and short-term intellectual development; and they demonstrate stronger and more positive social and emotional development.

If parent involvement is so beneficial for all involved (if it is implemented effectively), why then do so many schools and teachers neglect its importance? Greenberg (1989) outlines a number of reasons.

1. Some teachers and principals feel resentment toward parents. These resentments might revolve around jealousy rivalry, or the tension of having parents in such close proximity.

2. Some teachers have classist reactions. Feelings of inadequacy may emerge in teachers if the parents are of a higher educational or socioeconomic level. Conversely, feelings of superiority may emerge if the parents are of a lower educational or social status.

3. Some teachers may have feelings of exclusivity if they feel that because they have teaching credentials and parents don't, the parents should not be involved in or make educational decisions. This exemplifies the "we are the expert and they're not" attitude, often exclusively attributed to physicians and psychologists.

4. Some teachers feel protective of the children in their classroom. This feeling of attachment often leads to their not welcoming others' participation in the classroom.

5. While many teachers readily accept compliant parents, oftentimes teachers don't want to deal with parents who question, are insistent, are involved, or who are perceived as "pushy."

6. Some principals are protective of their school and don't want nonschool individuals involved.

PROMOTING PARENT INVOLVEMENT IN SCHOOLS

Although there are many obstacles that often stand in the way of implementing effective parent involvement opportunities, Greenberg (1989) also discusses the many ways in which the school can facilitate those opportunities. While not all of these strategies may be appropriate for all school settings, many of them can be incorporated into the public school educational process. Consider the following suggestions:

1. Build time into teachers' schedules for planning for parent involvement and for actually working with parents.
2. Encourage parents to become involved in making some school decisions after being instructed how to do so appropriately.
3. Encourage parents to study various early childhood education materials and curriculum approaches and to become involved in the selection process.
4. Listen to parents, knowing full well that they do not always agree with the school's position.
5. Hold parent meetings at various times of the day so that those with different schedules will have opportunities to participate.
6. Encourage parents to visit the school regularly and often, without an appointment.
7. Make special efforts to reach the hard-to reach-parents and give them a reason to come to the school.
8. Make an effort to get parents involved in child advocacy issues in the community.
9. Conduct meetings during which both parents and teachers together increase their understanding about children and how to increase their learning opportunities.
10. Encourage parents of all ability levels to help at their own skills level and make every effort to guarantee their comfort and success.
11. Whenever possible, put as many of the above suggestions that are appropriate in your classroom situation into daily practice.

Chapter 6

ONGOING EVALUATION AS A FACTOR IN DECISION MAKING AND CURRICULUM DEVELOPMENT

According to the National Association for the Education of Young Children (Bredekamp 1987), ongoing evaluation in early childhood education occurs primarily to determine the curricular needs of children. As noted in Chapter 4, there are others who have advocated that evaluation be used for purposes other than for determining curricular needs (e.g., Uphoff and Gilmore 1986), particularly in kindergarten. These others propose that children be evaluated to determine whether they are ready for school. A central assumption of the position of those who advocate this use of evaluation is that children should be grouped in school developmentally rather than by chronological age. Thus, if a child is of legal school entry age, but tests at a younger developmental age, that child presumably should be given the "gift of time," or another year, to become ready for the curriculum.

TESTING AND SCHOOL READINESS

The practice of testing to determine developmental level for the purpose of school entrance, in this author's opinion, constitutes both a class and a gender bias. Children from a background of economic poverty, and boys, in general, will be overidentified by developmental readiness instruments as those in need of the gift of time. Both socioeconomic status (SES) and sex have been shown to correlate with scores on tests such as these (Shepard and Smith 1988).

As has been discussed in an earlier chapter, the construction of knowledge, according to Piaget (Inhelder, Sinclair, and Bovet 1974), is the result of the interaction among the factors of maturation, physical and social experience, and equilibration. Although maturation is biologically determined, the remaining two factors are not. Therefore, a child's score on a developmental readiness test is only partially the result of the maturational process. Still, those who advocate the gift of time maintain that maturation alone—or time—is sufficient to bolster a child's developmental level and knowledge enough to ready him/her for kindergarten, even if the kindergarten curriculum is inappropriate.

Much of the variance of readiness test scores across groups of children is actually caused by the types of self-selected or societally selected experiences each child has had prior to taking the test. Thus, the belief of gift of time advocates that they are segregating out children who lack the appropriate maturational level necessary for success in early schooling is erroneous. They are also segregating out those who have not had the "appropriate" physical and social experiences that are required by most kindergarten curricula as measures of success—and in all likelihood, the kindergarten class may be the only place in which these children will receive these experiences.

Assessment instruments such as those used to determine gift of time children, look at development as though it can be photographed and scrutinized at that frozen moment in time. In essence these instruments ignore the child's past physical and social experiences that have influenced the responses. In addition, these tests cannot determine which type of experiences the child may require in the future, or how the child will benefit from those experiences.

EFFECTS OF SCHOOLING DECISIONS BASED ON GIFT OF TIME

Schooling decisions based on the gift of time may have various outcomes. One outcome is to prohibit children's entrance into kindergarten for an additional year. Another is to place children into what has come to be called a "developmental kindergarten," which is the first year of a two-year kindergarten track. These children will thus spend two years in kindergarten before they progress to first grade. Still another outcome of the gift of time is the transitional first grade. In this format, children identified as "not ready" will spend two years in first grade before progressing to second grade.

The schooling practice most often associated with the gift of time is the delay of children's entrance into kindergarten for an additional year. As with kindergarten entrance testing, this practice represents a classist and sexist bias, and has the potential for impeding the development of those children who are most in need of the experiences they will miss. This is particularly true for children who come from economic poverty, and for others who come from environments that do not afford them the types of experiences required for even modest success in today's schools.

It will be recalled that cognitive development is not only the product of maturation, but is also the product of the interplay of maturation with physical and social experiences. Children from economic poverty who are kept out of school for an additional year will probably not get the kinds of experiences they need to prepare them for school, whereas middle SES children may. Thus, by keeping such children out of school, the developmental gap between children from environments of relative advantage and disadvantage is likely to widen even more dramatically.

According to Kozol (1990), the practice of tracking children has similar effects. Children who are tracked into a two-year kindergarten or a transitional first grade are likely to be denied the experiences they require to advance. Such tracking is therefore, in essence, a type of segregation, implemented so that the poor in the lower tracks "cannot impede the progress of the more privileged children" (Kozol 1990, p. 52).

Devotees of schooling practices based on the gift of time believe that children are given the "gift" to allow them to mature and prepare them for a more successful early school experience. What these practices often constitute in reality is a "theft of time." This is particularly true for those children who *most* need the physical and social experiences that a developmentally appropriate kindergarten curriculum provides.

TEACHING, CURRICULUM, AND THE GIFT OF TIME

The gift of time phenomenon has the potential of adversely affecting not only children, but also the nature of the kindergarten and subsequent primary curriculum. By testing all children and excluding those whom an instrument deems not ready for kindergarten, we are engaging in the first step of "high-stakes testing" (Meisels 1988). According to Meisels, we are engaging in high-stakes testing if we are using tests to exclude children from kindergarten who are of legal entry age. Moreover, by including only those children in kindergarten who meet a given criterion level, we develop the potential for promoting an escalation of the kindergarten curriculum (Shepard and Smith 1988). It then follows that there will be an escalation of subsequent first, second, and third grade curricula as well. In this manner, the gift of time practices have resulted in the early childhood curriculum becoming test-driven and more academically oriented, another characteristic of high-stakes testing.

One outcome of this situation has been a steady increase in the average age of kindergarten children. This is occurring for two reasons. First, parents have been more likely to keep their children out of school for an additional year, so that their children are the "smartest" in the class. This tends primarily to be a middle-class phenomenon, to occur more with boys than with girls, and to occur most with summer-born children. Second, because of the escalation of the curriculum, more and more school districts are raising the minimum entry age for kindergarten. Between 1985 and 1989 twelve states have raised their kindergarten entry age (NAEYC 1989), some to as early as July (Shepard and Smith 1988). This constitutes another example of a "theft of time," particularly for those children who are in most need of the kindergarten experience. While middle-SES children may fill the year with preschool experiences or enriching experiences at home, many children from economic poverty will simply have to wait and thus lose more precious time. The vicious cycle of widening the academic gap between children of means and those of economic poverty, thus, continues.

The gift of time concept also has the potential effect of homogenizing both the kindergarten classroom and the curriculum. If only those children who are the most developmentally able are permitted into the kindergarten classroom, the result will be fewer numbers of children with individual differences and a corresponding type of curriculum. Teaching those children who are only the most developmentally ready makes teaching easier; therefore, this concept is getting support from some kindergarten teachers. This is especially true when teachers are pressured and the quality of their teaching ability is judged based on their class's standardized test performance.

THE RIGHT PROBLEM BUT THE WRONG SOLUTION

"Kindergarten requires children to sit quietly, to take turns, to work with workbooks and ditto sheets. But a lot of children at that age need more freedom to move around to play." According to Louise Bates Ames, one of the early proponents of the gift of time concept, this describes the kindergarten of today (Uphoff and Gilmore 1986, p. 31). Uphoff and Gilmore likewise lament that the typical contemporary kindergarten causes undo stress, lowers self-esteem, and creates other emotional and psychological problems in young children. Their solution is that "anyone under the age of five years, six months has no business in a formal classroom" (p. 6).

Most professionals in early childhood education would not argue with these positions, especially if a formal classroom means that every child must be doing the same thing at the same time, and must be instructed primarily in teacher-directed, large-group settings using worksheets and other like techniques. However, a formal classroom of this type has no business in kindergarten!

According to the gift of time advocates, the solution for reducing the stress imposed by kindergarten is to fix the children—that is, to give them more time so that they are better able to handle the stress. In this regard, they specifically contend that children below the age of five years, six months are simply not ready for kindergarten. However, it is not a matter of the child's readiness for kindergarten, but rather it's a matter of the kindergarten curriculum not being developmentally appropriate for children of legal entry age for school that should be taken into consideration.

Gift of time advocates also suggest that the younger children in kindergarten classrooms are being set up for failure. Their solution is to raise the kindergarten entry age. Shepard and Smith (1988) contend that raising the entry age merely exacerbates the curriculum problem. The effect of raising the average age of kindergarten children will surely result in a situation where even more will be "pushed down" into the curriculum from the higher grades. Again, the youngest will suffer. Raising the entrance age is not the solution for there will always be some who are the youngest in the class.

One cannot argue with the basic premises that (a) a bad start in school often leads to difficulty in school later; and (b) being required to perform at levels beyond one's developmental capabilities leads to stress, frustration, and low self-esteem. To this end the gift of time advocates make all the right points, identify all the right problems, but consistently come up with all the wrong solutions. The problem is not with the children, it is with the kindergarten curriculum.

The solutions to these problems are best put forth in the National Association for the Education of Young Children's (NAEYC 1988) position on what schools can do to ensure that all children get off to a sound start. They suggest the following:

70

1. That all children enter school on the basis of their chronological age and legal right to enter school, rather than on the basis of what they already know;
2. That teacher-child ratios should be low enough to allow teachers to individualize instruction and not expect that all children do the same thing at the same time;
3. That if children are grouped, the groupings should be flexible and change frequently so that the children don't have to conform to rigid expectations;
4. That children should be allowed to progress at their own pace through the curriculum;
5. That the curriculum and teaching methods be appropriate for the age and development of the children in the class.

EVALUATION FROM A DEVELOPMENTAL PERSPECTIVE

In the final statement listed above, the NAEYC states, in essence, that early childhood practices should reflect and take into account the child's level of development. As such, we should recognize the developmental characteristics of children and how they affect evaluation (Cryan 1986; Gullo 1988b, 1990b; Meisels 1987). It is imperative that the evaluation process be considered as an integral part of the curriculum in the early childhood classroom. As such there are a number of developmental concerns that should be considered in this process.

First, we should recognize the developmental constraints influencing children's responses in certain evaluative situations. When we assess whether a child during the early childhood years has acquired information during a particular instructional unit, we must not assume that an inappropriate response or no response at all indicates that the child does not have the information. One of the things that we should consider if this occurs is the developmental appropriateness of the method used to determine whether the child has the desired information.

If, for example, the method of assessment requires a child to exhibit extremely controlled fine-motor movements (e.g., fill in a small bubble on a sheet with many pictures and bubbles), to determine whether he/she has acquired some language or cognitive concept, the inability to exhibit controlled fine-motor movements may actually get in the way of his/her ability to demonstrate that he/she has acquired this knowledge.

If the language used to assess performance is unfamiliar to the child either due to an inappropriate level of development or to different experiential backgrounds, whether or not the child has the correct answer, if he/she did not understand the question, the child will not respond appropriately.

Another developmental characteristic of children during the early childhood years is that they demonstrate impulsive behaviors more frequently than children who are at more advanced levels of development. Impulsivity means that children will often respond with the first thing that comes to their mind, often without reflecting on alternatives. These reactions "without thinking" often lead younger children to respond inappropriately in assessment situations.

In summary, children's level of development—social, language, cognitive, motor, etc.—often determines how they will interpret and respond in evaluative situations. Therefore, we must take this into account when we interpret their responses.

Second, we should recognize that motivation to do well in evaluative situations differs, depending on the child's level of developmental accomplishments as well as on his/her experiential backgrounds. We know, both from our experience with children and youths, as well as from research, that motivation to do well in an evaluative situation partially accounts for one's performance in that situation. Young children often don't understand the importance or significance of their performance in situations, either formal or informal, where their knowledge is being assessed. Many times, the reinforcement or incentive to perform is simply to complete the task so that they can go on to a more comfortable, or to what they perceive to be a more enjoyable circumstance. There is little we can do, in general, to convince a five-, six-, or seven-year-old that how they perform

during certain evaluation settings may have long-range consequences for their academic future. It would also be folly to try to!
What we should be aware of, however, is that children's lack of
motivation to perform according to our expectations, due to their
developmental stage of understanding these types of circum-
stances, may influence their behavior.

In addition, there are some groups of children, in general,
who have more experience with "assessment-like" situations, and
therefore, may be more motivated at earlier ages than others to
perform well. Children who come from middle-SES homes are
more likely to have been engaged in these types of situations than
children who come from homes of economic poverty. Because
they are more likely to have had these types of experiences before,
with their parents, as well as in other types of settings, they may
exhibit more comfort with being asked questions, or being
assessed in other ways. Familiarity, alone, could account for these
children being more comfortable and therefore more motivated
to do well in an assessment situation.

Third, we should recognize that there are differences in
how children perceive themselves as compared to how others
perceive them related to their performance on various tasks. An
important element in the evaluation of children's performance is
the degree to which they incorporate feedback into the
internalized assessment of their own competence. Research
suggests that younger children misperceive their own competence when compared to teachers' ratings of their competence
(Gullo and Ambrose 1987; Stipek 1981). Teachers anticipate
that the critical feedback given to children is used by them to
gauge future behaviors. It is not clear that young children, below
the age of eight, perceive the feedback as criticism or that they use
teacher feedback aimed at academic competence to determine
future behaviors. Research has found that young children
uniformly have an exaggerated perception of their own abilities
(Gullo and Ambrose 1987; Stipek 1981). Nicholls (1978) found
that not until sixth grade do children's perceptions of their
abilities closely reflect their actual performance. Children's

ratings of their own performance do not begin to correlate with teacher ratings until about eight or nine years of age (Nicholls 1978, 1979).

A developmental explanation for this phenomenon exists. From a Piagetian framework, Stipek (1981) concludes that preoperational children may confuse the desire to be competent with reality. Because most children do not get feedback regarding their competence that is either all good or all bad, they are left with mixed messages as to what their actual performance status is. Preoperational children are then left to judge their own competency level based upon inconsistent and ambiguous feedback from the teacher. Piaget (1925) describes children of this age as having an exaggerated feeling of self-efficacy. This may be due to the egocentric nature of the preoperational child. Children at this age tend to concentrate on and pay attention to that which is salient to them. When they receive evaluative feedback from the environment, both positive and negative, they may focus on only the positive, thus getting a false sense of competence. Apple and King (1978) suggest that teachers of young children tend to focus on school behavior and social adjustment when they give feedback to the children rather than to provide reinforcement on the basis of the quality of the children's academic performance. The child may use this feedback to evaluate his or her competence in cognitive and academic performance as well. Thus, young children may get little direct and meaningful feedback regarding their academic performance.

Finally, we should recognize that there are differences in how children generalize their performance or knowledge from context to context. As was discussed in an earlier chapter, one cannot assume that because children can demonstrate knowledge or skills in one context, they will be able to generalize this knowledge or skill and thus be able to demonstrate it in all contexts. This is the vertical decalage phenomenon. If, for example, children are provided only with experiences with mathematical concepts and operations in contexts in which they manipulate objects but never have opportunities for using representational symbols, these children may not be able to demonstrate what they know when assessed representationally, with paper and pencil tasks. Therefore, it is imperative that children be given opportunities to experience knowledge and skills in many contexts, both concretely and representationally.

While it is true that children in the preoperational stage of development acquire new knowledge and skills when given concrete experiences with real objects, it is important that they be allowed to practice or generalize these newly acquired knowledge and skills in many contexts. The implication here is twofold. First, we must not assume that because a child can demonstrate knowledge or skill in a particular context, that he or she has complete understanding of this knowledge or skill enough to demonstrate it in all contexts. Second, we must not assume that because a child does not demonstrate knowledge or a skill in an evaluative setting, that he/she would not be able to demonstrate it given an appropriate context.

ALTERNATIVE ASSESSMENT

One way in which the field of early childhood education is addressing the issue of testing and assessment and the manner in which it fits into a curriculum that meets children's developmental needs is through alternative assessment. Alternative assessment is the term that is used to describe the types of assessment that are being used in lieu of, or in addition to, "standardized" testing procedures. These types of assessments are more descriptive in nature and take various forms. For example, some teachers use portfolios to chart children's progress. Portfolios are a systematic and organized collection of children's work. These collections are used as evidence to monitor the growth of students' knowledge, their skills, and their attitudes (Vavrus 1990).

Another type of alternative assessment is for the teacher to evaluate children's progress by assessing their knowledge and problem-solving skills through observing them in an actual problem-solving situation. "Project Spectrum" (Krechevsky 1991) is an example of one such assessment procedure.

Still another type of alternative assessment is the criterion-referenced behavioral checklist (e.g., Meisels and Steele 1991). The purpose of such checklists is for teachers to document children's progress in various skills and accomplishments, categorized according to certain curricular objectives. Teachers chart children's progress by observing their behaviors during classroom activities. The information is not used to compare one child to another, but rather, to describe a single child's growth over time.

Using alternative assessment has some distinct advantages:

1. This type of assessment procedure focuses on developmental changes. Thus, one can more easily identify progress.

2. There is a closer match between the curricular goals and assessment outcomes. Thus, the resulting information is more relevant.

3. These assessment procedures, if used appropriately, provide concrete and systematic means for curriculum modification.

4. These assessment procedures focus on the individual child rather than on groups of children. Thus, individualizing to meet children's needs is facilitated.

5. Alternative assessment procedures do not rely on the "one chance" opportunity for the child to demonstrate competence.

6. Alternative assessment procedures do not disrupt the process of curriculum implementation. Because these procedures are incorporated into the daily routine, the teaching-learning process is not interrupted.

7. Finally, alternative assessment procedures provide concrete information to present to parents.

Chapter 7

CONCLUSION

Much of the discussion in previous chapters focused on the importance of interaction in early childhood education. Many types of interactions were described explicitly or implied indirectly. The following interactions were addressed:

1. The importance of children's interactions with objects in their environment that are concrete, real, and relevant to their life experience;

2. The importance of children's interactions with other children and adults; and

3. The importance of children's interactions within the learning activities that meet curricular objectives.

More than an interactional approach to teaching in early childhood is required in order to achieve optimal learning and development in young children. What is called for is a transactional approach.

THE EARLY CHILDHOOD CURRICULUM:
A TRANSACTIONAL PROCESS

Transaction can be described as reciprocal interaction and mutual influence (Anastasiow 1986). In the early childhood education environment it implies that not only are the teacher, curriculum, and materials affecting the child, but the child should rightly be affecting the teaching that occurs, the curriculum that is developed, and the materials that are used to implement the curriculum.

The implications of this approach for early childhood education is that the teacher should take into account the biological development and experiential histories of each child in planning and implementing the curriculum. One should not expect that as the child interacts in the early childhood teaching-learning environment, that change will take place only on the part of the child. Rather, one should expect, that as children's individual differences are recognized, changes will occur in the implementation of the curriculum to accommodate those individual differences.

Recently, much is being said regarding the impact that children with disabilities or children with culturally, linguistically, or economically different backgrounds are having on early childhood education practices. From a transactional perspective, good early childhood practices would be appropriate for all children found in any one individual classroom. Certainly, there are children who are in need of specific types of intervention strategies. These children, too, are easily identified in a classroom that takes a transactional view of teaching and learning.

Yes, it takes work! It is easy to fall back and rely on a standardized early childhood curriculum, with an established scope and sequence, blaming the children if they find the "work" too hard. Yes, it is hard to accommodate individual differences in children through the curriculum. It is easier to have the children who may be "ahead" wait for the rest to catch up so that everybody can be at the same place at the same time.

Nobody ever said that teaching in early childhood was easy. Yes, it is hard. But . . . our children are worth the effort!

APPENDIX

TWO-WEEK INTEGRATED FARM UNIT: KINDERGARTEN LEVEL

Sample Parent Letter

Dear Parents:

Beginning next week, our unit for the next two weeks will be The Farm. The concepts that we will be working on are as follows:

1. recognizing farm animals;
2. animal sounds and noises;
3. animal babies;
4. animal houses and other farm buildings;
5. what farmers do;
6. what food grows on farms;
7. what happens to the food after it leaves the farm;
8. what animals eat.

It would be of great help if you have any magazines with pictures of things associated with the farm. It would be greatly appreciated if you could send them in or bring them into the classroom. I need these pictures for some of the activities that we will be doing in the Farm Unit.

Also, if you have not yet sent in your child's permission slip for our field trip to the farm, it needs to be returned to me by this coming Friday. If anyone would like to volunteer to accompany us on the field trip, the help would be greatly appreciated. The children seem to be very excited about our upcoming field trip, and I think that it will be a lot of fun!

Everyone is invited into our room at the end of our unit. We will have made a miniature farm, and the children will have stories to share.

I hope to see you soon. As always, thank you for your help and support.

Sincerely yours,

Mr. Gullo

Concept: Recognizing Farm Animals

Objective: Children will be able to recognize and distinguish between different farm animals.

Group Activities

Day 1: Read *Farm Animals* (Chicago: Children's Press, 1981). Discuss animals that are in the book.

Day 3: Play "Farm Yard Bingo." Children have bingo cards with pictures of farm animals on them. Teacher selects a picture of a farm animal. If the child has the animal on his or her card, he or she covers it with a marker.

Day 4: Field trip to the farm.

Day 9: Put together our classroom "Farm." Discuss the animals, buildings, and other things that will be part of our farm.

Day 10: Children can read or tell the class any of the stories they wrote during the Farm Unit.

Center Activities

Reading: **Days 1–10:** Have farm books available at the Reading/Language Center. Some examples include: *The Rooster Who Refused to Crow* (Troll Association, 1972); *This Farm Is a Mess* (Leslie McGuire, 1981); *Mr. Mac-a-doodle, You're a Genius* (Troll Associates, 1972); *Golly Gump Swallowed a Fly* (Parents' Magazine Press, 1981); *I Will Not Go to Market Today* (Dial Press, 1979); *Hello Farm Animals* (Troll Associates, 1985); *Animal Sounds* (Western Publishing Co. 1981).

Art: **Days 1–10:** Turn one table, one bulletin board, and sandbox into a farm. Day 1: make animals that live on farms; use paint, draw, and cut out, color, make with salt dough.

Math: **Days 1–3:** Sort pictures of alike animals into piles. Each pile will have five of the same type of animal.

Writing: **Days 1–3:** Children will write stories about farm animals using pictures, words, or both. These will be put on the Farm Bulletin Board.

Science: **Days 1–2:** Sorting farm and zoo animals. Children will select pictures of animals that live either on a farm or in the zoo. They will sort them by putting the farm animals in a barn and the zoo animals in a cage. The children can check their answers by looking on the back of the picture of the animal. If the animal is a farm animal, it will have a picture of a barn on it; if it is a zoo animal, it will have a picture of a cage on it.

Each day, during group time, the teacher will explain each of the new centers to the children.

Concept: Animal Sounds and Noises

Objective: Children will associate animals with the sounds that they make.

Group Activities

Day 2:   Teach the song "Farm Sounds." This is a song sung to the tune of "The Wheels on the Bus." (John Saltsman, Wenatchee, Wash.).

Day 3:   "Farm Yard Bingo." Children have bingo cards with pictures of farm animals. Teacher will select animal picture and make the sound that animal makes. If the children have that animal, they cover it up on the bingo card.

Day 4:   Field trip to a farm.

Day 5:   Give children pictures of baby or adult farm animals. When they hear the sound that the animal makes, the children match the baby with the adult animal.

Day 9:   Put together the class "Farm." Discuss noises while assembling the farm.

Center Activities

Listening: **Days 1–3:** Play a tape of "Old MacDonald." Have children match animal sounds to pictures of animals.

Math: **Days 3–5:** Flannel board and flannel groups of animals and sounds. Match the sound to pictures of animals. Each group of animals will have one animal, a group of two, etc., up to five animals. Match the correct number of animals to the correct number of sounds. For example, if the child hears four "baas," then match it to four sheep, etc.

Reading: **Day 2:** Add *Farm Yard Sounds* (Crown Publishers, 1986).

Concept: Farm Animals and Their Babies

Objective: Children will associate the baby farm animals with the adult animal.

Group Activities

Day 4: Read *Baby Animals on the Farm* (Kinderbuchver-lag Reich Luzern H.G., 1981).
Field trip to the farm.

Day 5: Give children pictures of baby or adult farm animals. The children divide into two groups, either of baby or adult animals. They take turns making the animal sound. The baby finds the parent animal by listening to the sound that it makes.

Day 9: Put together the class "Farm." Discuss the parent and baby animals including the names of each.

Center Activities

Art: **Day 3:** Have children make baby animals to go with the parent animal using the same materials for each pair.

Math: **Days 6–8:** Add flannel baby and parent farm animals. Match correct baby to the parent. Check to see if correct by turning over the pictures of animals. The same color on the back indicates that the match was correct.

Reading: **Day 4:** Add *Baby Animals on the Farm.*

Concept: Animal Houses and Other Farm Buildings

Objective: Children will be able to identify where certain animals live and name other types of buildings found on the farm.

Group Activities

Day 1: Read *Farm Animals*, (Chicago; Children's Press, 1981). Discuss houses that farm animals live in.

Day 4: Field trip to the farm.

Day 9: Put together class "Farm." Discuss the types of buildings that we are constructing. Put animals in their proper houses.

Day 10: Children can read or tell the class any of the stories that they wrote during the Farm Unit.

Center Activities

Blocks: **Day 1:** Add animals to the block area. Children can create houses for the animals along with other farm buildings.

Science: **Days 1–3:** *Animal Homes* (Kids' Stuff, Incentive Publications, 1969). On one-half of a flannel board, have pictures of farm animals with their names under the pictures. On the other half of the flannel board, have pictures of the animals' houses. Children will match the animal to the type of house that it lives in by taking different color strands of yarn and putting one end on the animal and the other end on the picture of the house.

Art: **Day 4:** Add material for children to make animals' houses and other buildings.

Writing: **Days 4–6:** Have children write stories about animals' life on the farm.

Concept: What Does a Farmer Do?

Objective: Children will be able to tell the various things the farmer does on the farm.

Group Activities

Day 4:   Read *Baby Animals on the Farm.*
Field trip to the farm.

Day 5:   Use flannel board. Have pictures of different kinds of activities. Have two categories on the flannel board: things that farmers do and things that farmers don't do. One at a time, each child will put a picture in the appropriate place. Discussion will take place following each child's placing of the picture.

Day 9:   Put together class "Farm." Discuss what farmers do on the farm during the activity.

Center Activities

Blocks: **Day 4:** Add farmer and the family to the block area. Children can have the farmer and the family do the activities that are generally done on the farm, through role play.

Art: **Day 6:** Have children make pictures of what farmers do. This activity can include making equipment that farmers use.

Listening: **Days 4–7:** Play an audiotape of things that farmers might say during their work on the farm and things that they would not say. Children will put pictures of what the farmer does on one side of a table, and pictures of what a farmer does not do on the other side of the table. At the end of the tape, it will tell the children what things the farmer does and what the farmer does not do. The children will then be able to check their answers.

Reading: **Day 5:** Add *Baby Animals on the Farm.*

Concept: Food Grown on the Farm and Where It Goes

Objective: The children will be able to recognize what types of food grow on a farm and describe what happens to it after it leaves the farm.

Group Activities

Day 4: Field trip to the farm.

Day 7: Show the film:"Where Does Our Food Come From?" (Coronet Films.) After viewing the film, the class will discuss it.

Day 8: Make a terrarium. Have children plant various vegetable seeds in the terrarium. Discuss how seed, grow into mature plants.

Day 9: Put together class "Farm." Discuss the different crops that are found on the farm and what happens to the harvested food.

Center Activities

Art: **Day 8:** Add equipment to the sand table (e.g., plows, tractors, etc., that the children made earlier). Children can turn the sand table into a pasture and then make "food" to plant in it.

Science: **Days 8–10:** Children will draw and cut out pictures of plants. They will divide them into fruits and vegetables (roots, stems, and leaves). They can also create a "new" food product that no one ever heard of.

Days 8–10: Children will match the pictures of food products with the animal that produces the food product. To check their answers, a picture of the animal from which the food product comes will be on the reverse side of the food picture.

Listening: **Days 8–10:** Add the album *The Grocery Store*, Bomar Records: "Sing a Song of Home, Neighborhood, and Community."

Concept: Foods That Farm Animals Eat

Objective: Children will be able to recognize that different animals eat different types of food. Children will be able to recognize the appropriate food for the various farm animals.

Group Activities

Day 1:   Read *Farm Animals* (Chicago: Children's Press, 1981). Discuss the food that animals eat.

Day 4:   Field trip to the farm.

Day 9:   Put together the class "Farm." Discuss what food animals eat while putting the farm together.

Day 10:   Children can read or tell the class any of the stories that they wrote.

Center Activities

Art: **Day 8:** Have children make food for the animals to eat out of various art media.

Math: **Days 9–10:** Match pictures of animals to pictures of food that they eat. Each animal will have a certain color on the back of the picture corresponding to the correct picture of food. Some food may go with more than one animal. These pictures will have both, or more, colors on the reverse.

Science: **Days 4–7:** Make a collage of animals and the different foods that they eat. Children can cut the pictures out of magazines or draw them.

Writing: **Days 7–9:** Have children write stories about animals and the food that they eat, or about where the food goes after it leaves the farm. The stories can be written using words or pictures.

REFERENCES

Anastasiow, N. J. *Development and Disability: A Psychobiological Analysis for Special Educators.* Baltimore: Brookes Publishing Co., 1986.

Apple M., and King, N. "What Do Schools Teach?" In *Qualitative Education: Concepts and Cases in Curriculum Criticism,* edited by G. Willis. Berkeley, Calif.: McCutchan Publishing Co., 1978.

Baratta-Lorton, M. *Mathematics Their Way.* Menlo Park, Calif.: Addison-Wesley Publishing Co., 1976.

Biber, B. *Early Education and Psychological Development.* New Haven: Yale University Press, 1984.

Bredekamp, S. *Developmentally Appropriate Practice in Early Childhood Programs Serving Children from Birth Through Age Eight.* Washington, D.C.: National Association for the Education of Young Children, 1987.

Broman, B. L. *The Early Years in Childhood Education.* Prospect Heights, Ill.: Waveland Press, 1989.

Cole, M.; Frankel, F.; and Sharpe, D. "Development of Free Recall Learning in Children." *Developmental Psychology* 4 (1971): 109–23.

Cryan, J. R. "Evaluation: Plague or Promise?" *Childhood Education* 62 (1986): 344–50.

Day, B., and Drake, K. *Early Childhood Education: Curriculum Organization and Classroom Management.* Alexandria, Va.: Association for Supervision and Curriculum Development, 1983.

Elkind, D. "Assessment in Early Childhood Education." Paper presented at the Annual Meeting of the National Association for the Education of Young Children, Washington, D.C., November 1990.

Epstein, J. L. "Building Parent-Teacher Relationships in Inner City Schools." *Family Resource Coalition Report* 2, no. 7 (1989).

Filmore, L. W. "Now or Later? Issues Related to the Early Education of Minority Group Children." Paper presented at the meeting of the Council of Chief State School Officers, Boston, August 1988.

Forman, G., and Kuschner, D. *The Child's Construction of Knowledge: Piaget for Teaching.* Washington, D.C.: NAEYC, 1983.

Gallagher, J., and Reid, D. *The Learning Theory of Piaget and Inhelder.* Monterey, Calif.: Brooks/Cole Publishing Co., 1981.

Garvey, C. *Play.* Cambridge, Mass.: Harvard University Press, 1977.

Ginsburg, H., and Opper, S. *Piaget's Theory of Intellectual Development: An Introduction.* Englewood Cliffs, N.J.: Prentice-Hall, 1978.

Gollin, E. S. "Factors Affecting the Visual Recognition of Incomplete Objects: A Comparative Investigation of Children and Adults." *Perceptual and Motor Skills* 15 (1962): 583–90.

Greenberg, P. "Parents as Partners in Young Children's Development and Education." *Young Children* 44, no. 4 (1989): 61–75.

Gullo, D. F. "Developmental Changes in Children's Thinking." In *Young Children in Context: Impact of Self, Family and Society on Development,* edited by C. S. McLoughlin and D. F. Gullo. Springfield, Ill.: Charles C. Thomas, 1985.

_____. "Guidelines for Facilitating Language Development." *Day Care and Early Education* 54 (1988a): 201–15.

_____. "Perspectives on Controversial Issues Related to Implementing the All-Day Kindergarten: Evaluation and Assessment." Paper presented at the Annual Meeting of the National Association for the Education of Young Children, Anaheim, Calif., November 1988b.

_____. "The Full-Day Kindergarten Expanding the Curriculum Horizontally." Paper presented at the Annual Meeting of the National Association for the Education of Young Children, Atlanta, November 1989.

_____. "The Changing Family Context: Implications for the Development of All-Day Kindergarten." *Young Children* 45, no. 4 (1990a): 35–39.

_____. "Assessment Issues in Early Childhood Education." Paper presented at the Early Childhood Leadership Retreat, Association for Supervision and Curriculum Development, Cincinnati, August 1990b.

_____. "The Effects of Gender, At-Risk Status and Number of Years in Preschool on Children's Academic Readiness." *Early Education and Development* (in press).

Gullo, D. F., and Ambrose, R. P. "Perceived Competence Social Acceptance in Kindergarten: Its Relationship to Academic Performance." *Journal of Educational Research* 8, no. 1 (1987): 28–32.

Gullo, D. F., and Bersani, C. "Effects of Three Experimental Conditions of Preschool Children's Ability to Coordinate Visual Perspective." *Perceptual and Motor Skills* 56 (1983): 675–78.

Gullo, D. F., and Burton, C. B. "Age of Entry, Preschool Experience, and Sex as Antecedents of Academic Readiness in Kindergarten." *Early Childhood Research Quarterly* (in press).

Hagen, J. W., and Hale, G. A. "The Development of Attention in Children." In *Minnesota Symposia on Child Psychology,* Vol. 2, edited by A. D. Pick. Minneapolis: University of Minnesota Press, 1973.

Harcourt, L. *Explorations.* Menlo Park, Calif.: Addison Wesley Publishing Co., 1988.

Hess, R. D.; Dickson, W. P.; Price, G. G.; and Leong, D. J. "Some Contrasts Between Mothers and Preschool Teachers in Interaction with Four-Year-Old Children." *American Educational Research Journal* 16 (1979): 307–16.

Hess, R. D.; Price, G. G.; Dickson, W. P.; and Conroy, M. "Different Roles for Mothers and Teachers: Contrasting Styles of Childcare." In *Advances in Early Education and Day Care,* Vol. 2, edited by S. Kilmore. Greenwich, Conn.: JAI Press, 1981.

Hochberg, J., and Brook, V. "Pictorial Recognition as an Unlearned Ability: A Study of One Child's Performance." *American Journal of Psychology* 2 (1962): 154–60.

Hudson, W. "Pictorial Depth Perception in Subcultural Groups in Africa." *Journal of Social Psychology* 52 (1960): 183–208.

————. "The Study of Pictorial Perception Among Unacculturated Groups." *International Journal of Psychology* 2 (1967): 90–107.

Inhelder, B.; Sinclair, H.; and Bovet, M. *Learning and the Development of Cognition.* Cambridge, Mass.: Harvard University Press, 1974.

Jackson, N. E.; Robinson, H. B.; and Dale, P. S. *Cognitive Development in Young Children.* Washington, D.C.: National Institute of Education, 1976.

Jones, E. *Dimensions of Teaching-Learning Environments.* Pasadena, Calif.: Pacific Oaks College, n.d.

Kaercher, D. "When It's Smart for a Youngster to Repeat a Grade." *Better Homes and Gardens,* June 1984, 21–23.

Kagan, J. "Individual Differences in the Resolution of Response Uncertainty." *Journal of Personality and Social Psychology* 2 (1965): 154–60.

————. "Do Infants Think?" *Scientific American* 226 (1972): 74–83.

Kail, L. J. *Memory Development in Children.* San Francisco: Freeman, 1979.

Kamii, C. "Leading Primary Education Towards Excellence: Beyond Worksheets and Drill." *Young Children* 40, no. 6 (1985): 3–9.

Katz, L. "Mothering and Teaching: Some Significant Distinctions." In *Current Topics in Early Childhood Education,* Vol. 3, edited by L. G. Katz. Norwood, N.J.: Ablex, 1980.

Kember, D., and Smith, L. B. "Is There a Developmental Trend from Integrality to Separability in Perception?" *Journal of Experimental Child Psychology* 26 (1979): 498–507.

Kemler, D. G. "Classification in Young and Retarded Children: The Primacy of Overall Similarity Relations." *Child Development* 53 (1982): 768–79.

Kozol, J. "The New Untouchables." *Newsweek,* Winter/Spring 1990, 48–53.

Krechevsky, M. "Project Spectrum: An Innovative Assessment Alternative." *Educational Leadership* 49 (February 1991): 43–48.

Krogh, S. *The Integrated Early Childhood Curriculum.* New York: McGraw Hill, 1990.

Leeper, S. H. *Good Schools for Young Children: A Guide for Working with Three-, Four-, and Five-Year-Old Children.* New York: Macmillan, 1974.

McGarry, T. P. "Integrating Learning for Young Children." *Educational Leadership* 44, no. 3 (1986): 64–66.

Markman, E. "Realizing That You Don't Understand: A Preliminary Investigation." *Child Development* 48 (1977): 986–92.

Meisels, S. J. "Uses and Abuses of Developmental Screening and School Readiness Testing." *Young Children* 42, nos. 4-6 (1987): 68–73.

———. "High Stakes Testing in Kindergarten." *Educational Leadership* 46, no. 7 (1988): 16–22.

Meisels, S. J., and Steele, D. M. *Early Childhood Developmental Checklist* (Field Trial Edition). Ann Arbor, Mich.: University of Michigan, 1991.

Morrison, G. S. *Parent Involvement in the Home, School and Community.* Columbus, Ohio: Merrill, 1978.

———. *Education and Development of Infants, Toddlers and Preschoolers.* Glenview, Ill.: Scott, Foresman and Co., 1988.

Mundy-Castle, A. C. "Pictorial Depth Perception in Ghanain Children." *International Journal of Psychology* 1 (1966): 290–300.

Mussen, P.; Conger, J.; Kagan, J.; and Huston, A. *Child Development and Personality.* New York: Harper and Row, 1984.

NAEYC. *Testing of Young Children: Concerns and Cautions.* Washington, D.C.: National Association for the Education of Young Children, 1988.

————. "Kindergarten Entry Ages." *The Early Childhood Advocate* 1, no. 1. Washington, D.C.: National Association for the Education of Young Children, 1989.

NASBE. *Right from the Start: The Report of the National Association of State Boards of Education on Early Childhood Education.* Alexandria, Va.: National Association of State Boards of Education, 1988.

Nicholls, J. "The Development of the Concept of Effort and Ability, Perceptions of Academic Attainment and the Understanding That Difficult Tasks Require More Ability." *Child Development* 49 (1978): 800–814.

————. "Development of Perception of Own Attainment and Casual Attributions for Success and Failure in Reading." *Journal of Educational Psychology* 71 (1979): 94–99.

Osborn, K., and Osborn, J. *Cognition in Early Childhood.* Athens, Ga.: Education Associates, 1983.

Oyemade, J.; Washington, V.; and Gullo, D. F. "The Relationship Between Head Start Family Involvement and the Economic and Social Self-Sufficiency of Head Start Families." *Journal of Negro Education* 58 (1989): 5–15.

Phillips, J. L. *The Origins of Intellect: Piaget's Theory.* San Francisco: Freeman Press, 1975.

Piaget, J. "De quelques formes primitives de causalite chez l'enfant." *L'anné e Psychologique* 26 (1925): 31–71.

————. *The Moral Judgement of the Child.* New York: Macmillan, 1955.

_____ . *The Origins of Intelligence in Children.* New York: Norton Library, 1963.

Piaget, J., and Inhelder, B. *The Psychology of the Child,* translated by H. Weaver. New York: Basic Books, 1969.

Pick, A.D. "Improvement of Visual and Tactual Form Discrimination." *Journal of Experimental Psychology* 69 (1965): 331–39.

Pick, A. D.; Christy, M. D.; and Frankel, G. W. "Developmental Study of Visual Selective Attention." *Journal of Experimental Child Psychology* 14 (1972): 166–75.

Pick, A. D.; Frankel, D. G.; and Hess, V. L. "Children's Attention: The Development of Selectivity." In *Review of Child Development,* Vol. 5, edited by E. M. Hetherington. Chicago: University of Chicago Press, 1976.

Powell, D. *Families and Early Childhood Programs.* Washington, D.C.: National Association for the Education of Young Children, 1989.

Rogers, D. L., and Ross, D. D. "Encouraging Positive Social Interaction Among Young Children." *Young Children* 40, no. 6 (1986): 59–64.

Scarr, S. "An Evolutionary Perspective on Infant Intelligence. Species Patterns and Individual Variations." In *Origins of Intelligence: Infancy and Early Childhood,* edited by M. Lewis. New York: Plenum Press, 1976.

Schickendanz, J. "More Than the ABC's: The Early Stages of Reading and Writing." Washington, D.C.: National Association for the Education of Young Children, 1986.

Seefeldt, C., and Barbour, N. *Early Childhood Education: An Introduction.* Columbus, Ohio: Merrill, 1990.

Shepard, L. A., and Smith, M. L. "Escalating Academic Demand in Kindergarten: Counterproductive Policies." *Elementary School Journal* 89 (1988): 135–45.

Spodek, B. *Teaching in the Early Years* Englewood Cliffs, N.J.: Prentice-Hall, 1985.

Stipek, D. J. "Children's Perceptions of Their Own and Their Classmates' Ability." *Journal of Educational Psychology* 73 (1981): 404–10.

Uphoff, J., and Gilmore, J. E. *Summer Children: Ready or Not for School.* Middletown, Ohio: J & J Publishing, 1986.

Vavrus, L. "Put Portfolios to the Test." *Instructor* (August 1990): 48–51.

Weaver, P. "Children Starting Kindergarten Early Are More Likely to Fail School." *The National Enquirer,* October 1985.

Yussen, S. R., and Santrock, J. W. *Child Development: An Introduction.* Dubuque, Iowa: W. C. Brown Co., 1982.